# WAITING ON GOD

*Elena Radef*

# WAITING ON GOD

## HOW PATIENCE CREATES PRAYERS WITH IMPACT

# ELENA RADEF

*Waiting on God* by Elena Radef
Copyright © 2022 by Elena Radef
www.elenaradef.org
All Rights Reserved.
ISBN: 978-1-59755-697-2
All rights reserved

Published by:   ADVANTAGE BOOKS™
                Longwood, Florida, USA
                www.advbookstore.com

This book and parts thereof may not be reproduced in any form, stored in a retrieval system or transmitted in any form by any means (electronic, mechanical, photocopy, recording or otherwise) without prior written permission of the author, except as provided by United States of America copyright law.

Scripture taken from the Amplified Bible (AMPCE), Copyright © 1954, 1958, 1962, 1964, 1965, 1987 by The Lockman Foundation. Used by permission.

Library of Congress Catalog Number: 2022943286

| | |
|---|---|
| **Name:** | Radef, Elena, Author |
| **Title:** | *Waiting On God: How Patience Creates Prayers with Impact* |
| | Elena Radef |
| | Advantage Books, 2022 |
| **Identifiers:** | ISBN (print): 978159755672 |
| | (mobi, epub): 9781597557047 |
| **Subjects:** | Christian Life: Inspirational |

First Printing: October 2022
22 23 24 25 26 27    10 9 8 7 6 5 4 3 2 1

# Table of Contents

**PREFACE** .................................................................................. 7

## THE IMPORTANCE OF PRAYER

**1: WHAT IS THE TABERNACLE OF TODAY?** ................................. 9

**2: THE POSITION OF A CHILDLIKE HEART** ................................. 19

**3: THE IMPORTANCE OF HAVING THE FEAR OF GOD** ................. 25

**4: HARD TO PRAY** .................................................................. 35

**5: THE IMPACT OF WORDS** ..................................................... 41

**6: UNDERSTANDING HUMILITY** ............................................... 47

**7: UNDERSTANDING GOD IS OUR REFUGE** ............................... 55

**8: TAKING ON THE LIKENESS OF JESUS** ................................... 67

## HOW TO GROW IN THE LIKENESS OF JESUS

**9: WALKING IN GOD'S POWER** ................................................ 71

**10: IMPATIENCE, WORRY, AND FEAR MAKE US WITHDRAW** ....... 75

**11: UNDERSTANDING THE RIGHTEOUSNESS OF GOD** ................ 83

**12: KNOWING GOD IS OMNIPRESENT** ..................................... 87

**13: THE IMPACT OF THE PSYCHOLOGICAL INFLUENCE FROM THE PAST** .................... 91

## THE REALITY OF INTIMATE PRAYER LIFE

**14: UNDERSTANDING THE INTIMATE PRAYER LIFE** ..................... 95

**15: WHAT ARE INTERCESSORY PRAYERS** ................................. 103

**16: GROWING IN THE INTIMATE RELATIONSHIP WITH GOD** ........ 109

**APPENDIX** ............................................................................ 167

*Elena Radef*

# **Preface**

As we all know, the Bible contains many layers. All scripture referred to in this book is just one layer of the Bible. Utilizing the scriptures as done in this book doesn't mean that this is the only way to understand that scripture. God has set up the Bible with many layers, which is one of the amazing things about it. It is one of the reasons why we can continually receive deeper revelation from God's Word.

In this book, the reference of scripture is to the inner personal prayer and not so much so the community of prayer, praying in groups and prayer in church, yet exclaiming that we need a church to go to, and we need the community of fellowship to be in; never to abandon this very important fact. However, in reference to this book, it would require too much space and work to address these facts in each subject constantly. Therefore, take it as a given that all Christian people know of the importance thereof, and therefore it is no need to address it continually.

*Elena Radef*

# THE IMPORTANCE OF PRAYER

## Chapter 1

## What is the Tabernacle of Today?

**The inner holy tabernacle of God**

Prayer always has and will be a primary trait of our Christian walk with God. It is one of the most outspoken occurrences in the Bible, with people doing and practicing it all the time throughout the Bible. It was a lifestyle for all people in the Bible. It is the way to have communion with the Lord. Not just to hear what He says but to commune with Him, knowing what's on His heart and knowing Him intimately, into-me-see life with Him. Not just for us to see Him but also for making ourselves available to Him in a way that we are not trying to hide anything from Him. In this way, the openness and close intimate friendship with Him flourish in knowing each other well.

We must return to this type of relationship and restore it in today's church. Unfortunately, many churches preach the Old Testament of works, not the New Testament, the Covenant of Grace. Still trying to make the Christian people work for the grace of God. The result is that the church has lost the intimate prayer life with God. The result is the condition of today's church (failing and hurting Christians; people leaving churches; non-Spirit-filled churches, but sad to say; churches that are filled with the other spirit moving and) taking over. Many stay in church for a long time until they reach a point of frustration before realizing the foundation of a deep-rooted relationship with the Lord is not there. They recognize that nothing is rooting or bringing new life to the church. In other words: no awakening. The church is so much in control that even though the Lord left it many years ago, the church doesn't even know it. What has taken over in the church is the devil; the church is merely being fed spiritually with superficial nonsense, not something that makes one spiritually mature. This condition is especially moving in the western churches; the richer the nation is, the worse this tendency is.

All of this has to be restored, made whole, and healed in the church and The Holy Tabernacle of God has to be reinstalled and restored in the church. This comes by living the intimate prayer life with Jesus. In the Old Testament, it is depicted as the Tabernacle. It is partially fulfilled in the New Testament, and the complete fulfillment is in the end times.

There has always been a place for people to commune with the Lord, and this is the place. Only the priest was allowed to go into the Holy of Holies in the Old Testament. In the New Testament, we have all become priests and now have access because of the tearing down of the veil, which Jesus did on the Cross. When Jesus died on the Cross, all that was dead and unable to function was brought back to life. That includes us as well (Matt. 5:17). So many miraculous things happened; the most miraculous one was for us to be able to come boldly to the throne of our Father through Jesus, to enter into communion with God. We are unable to come near to comprehend its greatness. Yet we are still not living in its fullness and will not be able to until we are in heaven because this physical body hinders us from receiving the full revelation. It was not meant for us to understand fully now. But while on earth, we get a foretaste of what is to come, a communion with God that we cannot imagine; this Jesus made available for us.

> *And Jesus cried again with a loud voice and gave up His spirit. And at once the curtain of the sanctuary of the temple was torn in two from top to bottom; the earth shook and the rocks were split. The tombs were opened and many bodies of the saints who had fallen asleep in death we raised [to life]; And coming out of the tombs after His resurrection, they went into the holy city and appeared to many people. (Matthew 27: 50-53)*

Now we wear the garment of the priesthood, and there is no longer any difference between man and women or human positional order. We are all equal to enter into the Throne room of God (Gal. 3:28).

Everything in the Tabernacle is a picture of what we have access to and how; therefore, it is no longer a mystery; everything in the Tabernacle has a meaning for our prayer life. The revelation of the tabernacle is now available. Spending time with the Lord to make us receive the revelations in our prayer; is the part each of us must understand the necessity of. We cannot copy somebody else's revelation and think we get it because they have it. We must each of us receive the revelations directly from the Holy Spirit. These revelations come from spending time with the Lord; out of this, we get to know what is on His mind and heart through the unction of the Spirit, an outpouring combined with revelation. This is how we know if the Spirit moves us, it always brings forth revelation. Thus, the revelations we receive should always be biblical.

The mercy seat in the Old Testament is the analogy of the place where God spoke of Moses and told him about the commandments and how to lead the people. For us today, this means we are all called to hear from the Lord, finding out how to be led by the Lord in every situation in life through our prayer life. This is where God speaks to us, in the Holy of Holies in our inner chamber. Jesus' work on the Cross and the work of the Holy Spirit after His resurrection made it possible for us to enter the Holy of Holies without any intermediaries.

The communion we see displayed in the Old Testament always followed after the Lord had spoken, and reconciliation was the purpose of the Old Testament. Communion for us after the Cross is remembering what Jesus did on the Cross, and because of the great Passion, the purpose for full and lasting reconciliation is available. He fulfilled the reconciliation with the Father, enabling us to come boldly to the throne room. He tore down the veil for us and made a lasting reconciliation.

The Mercy Seat with the cherubim is a picture of God being the One who is watching over everything eternally; God sees everything. The eyes are a picture of knowledge. The Bible tells us to let them that have an ear to hear and eyes to see in order to understand (Rev. 2:7, 2:11, 2:17, 2:29, 3:6,

3:13, 3:22). To receive understanding, we must learn to see and hear spiritually what goes on. Out of this, we receive wisdom, knowledge, and understanding. That knowledge and wisdom do not come through the ways of the world but through turning our attention to the Lord, seeking His face.

> *And you shall make a mercy seat (a covering) of pure gold, two cubits and a half long and a cubit and a half wide. And you shall make two cherubim (winged angelic figures) of [solid] hammered gold on the two ends of the mercy seat. Make one cherub on each end, making the cherubim of one piece with the mercy seat, on the two ends of it. And the cherubim shall spread out their wings above, covering the mercy seat with their wings, facing each other and looking down toward the mercy seat. You shall put the mercy seat on the top of the ark and in the ark, you shall put the Testimony [the Ten Commandments] that I will give to you. There I will meet with you and, from above the mercy seat, from between the two cherubim that are upon the ark of the Testimony, I will speak intimately with you of all which I will give you in commandment to the Israelites. (Exodus 25:17-22)*

The meaning of the word Ark resembles the following: gathering, put together, derived from the word to gather, pluck, pick; also means something that affords protection and safety. That sums up the meaning of why the Ark contained such great importance to the Israelites. For us today, it sums up the Lord's purpose for our lives, which has come to pass through the redeemed work of Jesus Christ. The lid on the Ark is the Mercy seat, which resembles the following:

- Mercy.
- A blessing that is an act of divine favor or compassion.
- A place to rest and to be sure to be held in safety.

In combining these two, the Ark and the Mercy seat, we receive a revelation on the meaning of it, and we quickly understand that Jesus made it possible for us to sit down and rest, be protected, and no longer orphans but children gathered up and residing in His house because He fulfilled the promises. In the Old Testament, the commandments were only made for the Israelites. The gentiles were not invited to the table. But, through the redeemed work of Christ, we are now all invited.

The tabernacle of today is our prayer time with the Lord. We no longer need a physical place to go to. The Mercy Seat was where the Lord came and spoke to His people through the priest, Moses (Num. 7:89), David, and so forth, but still only for some. They were a foreshadowing of turning to the Lord in prayer. They served a purpose, which summarizes a fully installed prayer life, only enabled for all, through Christ. We no longer need to go into the physical place of the Mercy Seat; now, we can turn our face toward the face of Christ in our hearts. The outer tabernacle has become the inner tabernacle of Christ through the Holy Spirit.

A remark regarding David and the Ark of the covenant: the Lord used him to install worship for all. Thus all are invited to the tent. He set up a tent of meeting through the fact that he was not invited to the tabernacle of Moses because he was illegitimate. Because he was born of a mother through iniquity and sin, he was a foreshadow of how we should and could, despite being outsiders, come and be able to worship the Lord. The importance for us today regarding the tabernacle of David is that the Lord will return and rebuild the tabernacle of David, all through which the rest of mankind will seek the Lord (Acts 15:16-17). There is, therefore, a reason to understand the depth of the spiritual meaning of the tabernacle of David in regards to prayer. He spoke to the Lord within and yet honoring the Ark of the Covenant, the precepts and orders of God, yet he was only able to fulfill some parts. Likewise, Moses, Joshua, and the rest of the numerous people that God installed for different purposes; all honored the Lord in the Holy Tabernacle. They sought the Lord for all affairs in life, and they dared not to act without having communed with Him. He was picturing the importance of spending time with the Lord.

However, there was only One who could fulfill them all, Jesus. Being part of the Bible, they all were a foreshadow of Jesus, summarized in Him. In the Tabernacle, God spoke to His people, leading and preserving them. This is the analogy of communing with the Lord in prayer: God is a speaking God. He confides all things to us. The analogy is the loving relationship: the ones we love, we share all that is within. When God speaks, He is watching over His commandments, leading in His commandments. Therefore, all He speaks would always need to be traced back to His commandments; this is the life He has called us to live and abide in because it is the only right way of living.

And by the great display of His love for us which occurred on the Cross; Him giving Jesus, we are then enabled to share our secrets and our faults without being condemned. We want to share our faults because we have now known and understood man's carnal, sinful nature. With this knowledge, there arises freedom to share our faults and agony in the Light of Christ. Since He is the Light of the World, no darkness can abide in His presence. Therefore, when we confide in Him, He molds the darkness within into Light.

We come to understand the life He holds in all affairs throughout His names: Elohim – Mighty Creator, Abba–Father, Jehovah-Jireh - our provider, Elohim-Shomri - our projector, Parakletos - our advocate, Jehovah-Nissi - our banner, Jehovah-Rapha - our healer, Adonia - our Master, Jehovah-Shalom – our Lord of peace, El Shaddai - our all-sufficient one God almighty, etc.

In the inner tabernacle, all spiritual qualities are satisfied so we can live and follow the noble path of Christ: The Seven golden stick lampstand, the Menorah, symbolizes the providing light to keep us on our path. Only God's light, insight, and directions will keep us on the right track. In the spiritual realm, we will experience the physical presence of God's light. It overshadows us and gives us protection. That explains why Moses and Jesus could fast for forty days and night. The light of God does not only light up our path but also provides the physical need for us to stand trials. In the beginning, God said let there be light, and the light was brought forth, and out of that light, life came into existence. This happens with our inner man when in the presence of God's light. We are not only sustained and upheld, but we also come to life.

Seven is the number that means in full, completeness, and perfection. There are numerous references to the number seven throughout the Bible, especially in the book of Revelation, where it is mentioned 54 times. Throughout the Bible, the word seven is mentioned 735 times, and it depicts the Lord making a unblemished bride that He will come back to molded through His image.

It tells us of His perfection, and things take form out of that perfection and completion. This is the way He moves, and this is the way He deals with all situations - through the perfection in Him. Perfection also means that there is nothing that misses His attention and that in everything He does, the situation turns into a perfect ending, which means it ends in completeness.

Perfection means without fault or defect. It also means accurate, pure, total, absolute, and sane. This describes the place He longs for us to be in very well, and this residing place is only found in Him.

We shall receive in full in the Holy of Holies; we won't lack. On the contrary, we shall receive abundantly. He came so that we may have an abundant, rich life here on earth, understanding that He is the riches of life. He is the abundance we are all searching for because He says I came that they may have life more abundantly. (Joh. 10:10).

The Shewbread – means "bread of presence" in Hebrew. The cakes were made as an offering to God in the Old Testament. That depicts very well what we become in eating the body of Christ. He is the source of all life; we must come to the source to gain true life. We must eat the body of Christ to become like Jesus because it is only through Him life consist (Joh. 6:51-57). And when doing so, we become the shewbread offering for God. When we enter the Holy of Holies on the inner, we feed on God.

> *And the tempter came and said to Him, If you are God's Son, command these stones to be made [loaves of] bread. But He replied, It has been written, Man shall not live and be upheld and sustained by bread alone, but by every word that comes forth from the mouth of God. (Matthew 4:3-4)*

Interestingly, the tempter tells Jesus to turn the stones to bread in asking Him if You are the Son of God. The connection between the question and answer proves the exact point; that every Word of God sustains us because

Jesus' response is that man is to live by every Word that proceeds from the mouth of God (Deut. 8:3). And since Jesus is the Word, He becomes the bread of life that we must eat.

This is how Jesus was sustained in the wilderness through the Word of God. Every time Jesus answers a question, He provides a key that unlocks understanding. Here He unlocks the spiritual question of how He was sustained and how we are sustained by believing in Him and the Word.

The Oil – is the anointing being poured over our lives in the presence of God. We need anointing to execute the different tasks that God gives us, and we need anointing to stand in the evil day, which is referred to as testing and trials.

When we undergo trials and testing, we become the sweet-smelling sacrifice for God. The occurrence of Mary pouring perfume on the feet of Jesus before His great passion was how the occurrence of Him giving up His life for us became even more beautiful. He was anointed to become a well-smelling sacrifice before God (Joh. 12:1-3). There must be the breaking of the alabaster box, testing, and trials before the oil can be poured out; before anointing can flow (Matt. 26:7, Mrk. 14:3, Luk. 7: 36).

The Rod – teaches us that God chose Aaron's rod, among others, to put an end to the rebellion that was moving among the Israelites. God made it plain and simple so that no one could miss out that it was all the workings of the Lord. In that same moment when Aaron's rod budded, everyone knew that he was the one God had chosen to carry the authority needed. This same occurs for us when we spend time in His presence; it molds us to be able to carry the authority from God. Here very clearly stated that the authority came from God and can only come from God, and the way He is making a display of how He is doing it puts an end to all opposition and murmuring. There will always be people murmuring and opposing what God is doing in our lives, and like in this incident, God made it very clear that it was not something Aaron thought of as a good idea, but it came from God. This means the things God is making us in charge of, that everyone will at some point recognize that the authority installed is from God (Num. 17:1-11).

The Tablets – the ten commandments from God. A constant reminder for the Israelites not to forget that God set up the Law. What they needed to obey in order not to offend God. Very strict and precise. So much work and precision that no one could keep the Law but Jesus. This, of course, is the realization the Israelites should have come to terms with; we need a Savior.

In prayer, we come very quickly to terms with that we cannot fulfill the Law, but through the grace of God, we can, because of the fulfilling of the redemption of Jesus Christ for our lives, because He fulfilled the Law.

The Manna – was a constant reminder for the Israelites that God provided and sustained them, and the fact that they ate manna for forty years shows the Lord's sovereignty. God told the Israelites to place the manna before Him in the tent of testimony so that generations to come would be preserved (Exo. 16:33-35). They can only be preserved in the knowledge of God being their provider. Again, God is displaying to us that we need a Savior. This realization we come to abide in when spending time in His presence. The Lord knows that we are in need of knowing that it is by Him we are provided for and sustained. This revelation is poured into us in His presence in the Most Holy place.

The Golden Altar of incense – in the Old Testament, the offering of incense took place after the sacrifice. For us today, that means our sacrifices for the Lord will mount up as beautiful incense before the Father. A sacrifice is something we surrender and give in exchange for what the Lord has in store for us. These sacrifices we hand over to Him in prayer, and we seek His face for answers to our problems.

*Elena Radef*

# Chapter 2

# The Position of a Childlike Heart

**The innocence of a purged heart; being on fire for Him**

In prayer, it is important to approach the Lord in a true manner. True means understanding how to position ourselves on the inner, which is to find the door of the heart and then know how to enter through it. The Lord carries a personality that truly deserves our honor; His requirement for us is to approach Him with a childlike heart. In contemplating and reading this, we come to fathom that we by ourselves cannot approach Him in a true manner. By this, we fathom that we need Him to do that. We must come to terms with that when we approach Him. It is not something we can grasp through the carnal man because it is not of the carnal man. But as for approaching the Lord, we must lose sight of ourselves and make ourselves available as an open vessel in which He can pour Himself. In this manner, our heart's position needs to be like that of a child: open, vulnerable, and free from opinions. We must be receptive to receiving what He offers to pour through us. This centrality of a childlike heart we see throughout the whole Bible.

Touching on the topic in the deepest and most delicate way to comprehend how important the matter is; makes it crucially important to understand because we could very easily miss the delicate, sweet tenderness of the Holy Spirit and never be able to enter the door of the heart.

The Holy Spirit needs for us to wait to let Him be able to work His way through the obstruction of the carnal man. Doing this requires time soaking in His presence. The soaking prepares us to become able to be the vessels He can use. Soaking is the first step to sinking deeper in. If we don't know how to be soaked in His presence, we will stay outside of the inner position of the Holy of Holies in the heart. This circle of being soaked first to go deeper into the Holy of Holies is always ongoing. This is the nature of the workings of the Holy Spirit. In the soaking, the Holy Spirit is teaching us to become like Him, sweet, tender, delicate, all in order to be led by Him in prayer and life. By this, our life and prayer have no separation.

Misconceptions about what it means to approach Him in a true manner must be dealt with. What does it mean to do right? So many think of this matter from the carnal man's perspective, which is useless. As discussed, so many fail to understand what it means to approach Him in a true manner. There is an emphasis on the carnal man and not on God. Far too many think from the perspective of the carnal man in approaching the Lord, moving from an appropriate carnal behavior, which is the exact reason why many difficulties arise in growing a proper prayer life.

Understanding and performing through the carnal man only produce condemnation and no growth. It produces contrary to what is wanted and needed result; only leanness of soul and growth in pride. By this, we experience fatigue in the soul. The fatigue sucks the life out of the soul and creates a slow decaying of the soul as if one is powerless even to do the most basic things. We become lifeless. We can experience being dry in the soul through a cleansing process, but that is of a different nature.

In trying to understand the nature of prayer through the carnal man, we must fully understand that this perspective of a prayer life is of the Old Law where man worked His way into the presence of God. We must grasp that we are under the New Law, which is the Covenant of Grace; works all done and finished by Jesus Christ.

> *At that time, the disciples came up and asked Jesus, Who then is [really] the greatest in the kingdom of heaven? And He called a little child to Himself and put him in the midst of them, And said, Truly I say to you, unless you repent (change, turn about) and become like little children [trusting, lowly, loving, forgiving], you can never enter the kingdom of heaven [at all]. Whoever will humble himself therefore and become like this little child [trusting, lowly, loving, forgiving] is greatest in the kingdom of heaven. (Matthew 18:1-4)*

We have to turn and repent from the works of the old lifestyle, the Old Testament, and we have to turn to the new lifestyle of grace, the New Testament, which we receive through Jesus. We cannot fathom this by the nature of man. We must accept Jesus as our Savior so that the Holy Spirit can come and abide within us. The nature of man does not carry a childlike heart. Only the Spirit of God Jesus carries the childlike heart that He is addressing. That means in everything we need to become or do, we can only achieve it through Jesus, the birth of a new heart (Ezek. 36:26). Everything within is birthed anew when we receive the Lord Jesus as our Savior (Joh. 3:3).

What comes out of our mouth is what abides in our hearts, and by carrying the lowly nature of man, we can see what springs forth: the lowly, carnal, opinionated affairs that keep the carnal man in bondage (Matt. 15:18-20). Therefore, the heart of the carnal man needs to be purged so that we can let the righteous heart of God be installed within us.

The heart is the central theme for God when He is looking upon our lives. It is of the utmost importance for Him, in consideration for our sake for us to run our race well. We see this theme of importance over and over in the Bible. Noah, Moses, David, Ester, Ruth, and Daniel all underwent purgation to refine their hearts so that they would be of service to the Lord. The Lord cares that we will be able to stand on the evil day, all to endure for His name's sake.

By this, we also see in the Bible why people fell away from the Lord; again, it was a matter of the heart's position. As in the cases of Solomon, Saul, and Judas. They were all led by the nature of the carnal man.

> *Then little children were brought to Jesus, that He might put His hands on them and pray; but the disciples rebuked those who brought them. But He said, Leave the children alone! Allow the little ones to come to Me, and do not forbid or restrain or hinder them, for such [as these] is the kingdom of heaven composed. (Matthew 19:13-14)*

What an excellent analogy of how His ways are very different from how we think. We hardly recognize what is of the utmost importance to Him (the children). We hardly recognize the importance of a childlike heart. The most valuable quality for God is that we are humble, contrary to the world's most valuable quality; what we become and do. Time in His presence molds us to become like Him, and by this, what He thinks is important.

> *In that same hour He rejoiced and gloried in the Holy Spirit and said, I thank You Father, Lord of heaven and earth, that You have concealed these things [relating to salvation] from the wise and understanding and learned, and revealed them unto babes (the childish, unskilled, and untaught). Yes, Father, for such was Your gracious will and choice and good pleasure. (Luke 10:21)*

Clearly stated, it will become impossible for us to receive any revelation from God unless we carry a childlike heart. It is the will of the Father for it to be like this, it is not something we can alter in any way, and it is, in fact, a criterion. Jesus is talking to people living under the Old Testament, referring to the fact that the Pharisees did not understand the revelation that they needed a Savior. They understood the Old Testament Law, and that was the lifestyle lived. That means they knew the Law, and therefore they considered themselves being "right." Through this, they became full of themselves and lost the innocence of their heart. We can only receive teaching and training when we are freed from opinions and constantly dare to be in a heart position of letting prefixed understanding be taken aside. In this place, there is an open space in the heart to receive. It becomes a picture of when we think we know what is right and wrong, what to do, and when to do it. We are in that being full of ourselves without confiding in God first. As a result, we lose the innocence of the heart and our relationship with Him. We cannot hear and see in the spiritual when we are full of ourselves and the ways of the world, and that's what the Pharisees represent in this scripture. This also applies during communion with the Lord; we cannot tell Him how to mold us in prayer. The steps He is taking each of us through vary somewhat, depending on how we need to change and grow. Yet Christ has some foundational traits that He molds within our hearts, but the order varies in how He is doing it. Therefore, we must understand the importance of being open toward His presence in prayer, letting Him do the molding, and letting Him take us through the purgation in prayer time.

> *And they kept bringing young children to Him that He might touch them, and the disciples were reproving them [for it], But when Jesus saw [it], He was indignant and pained and said to them, Allow the children to come to Me - do not forbid or prevent or hinder them-for to such belongs the kingdom of God. Truly I tell you, whoever does not receive and accept and welcome the kingdom of God like a little child [does] positively shall not enter it at all. (Mark 10:13-15)*

Here we see how He talks about how we should receive others with a childlike heart, which we can only be understood by carrying a childlike heart ourselves. The way God is leading us in the Spirit requires that we are open at heart, just like a child. That's how He wants to move within each of us to make us grow spiritually. Reaching others requires that we don't carry prefixed ideas about Him and the way He is doing things; then clearly understand and see why He is so keen on and is looking out for our heart's position. Nobody understood what Jesus said and did in the Old Testament because none of them were Holy Spirit-filled people. The revelation they should have received was that we all need a Savior. This analogy for us today is that we need Jesus to alter and change our hearts.

*Elena Radef*

# Chapter 3

# The Importance of Having the Fear of God

**The reverential fear of God is the love for God**

God created us as individuals, and we are still individually unique in heaven. The fact that each of us was made as individuals with our own unique character traits is to be thought of as God showing Himself in each of us in different ways. Therefore, He needs all of us. We are all important to Him. Otherwise, something would be missing in Him. Likewise, when considering ourselves as parents, we are whole within but not complete as a parent without our children.

Therefore, each of us is of utmost importance to Him. His main aim is that we will be purged, sanctified, and receive the life of living in an intimate relationship with Him before going to heaven because it directly affects us in the afterlife.

The soul never dies. This is the reality we must come to understand, and it is the main purpose of coming home into the kingdom of God to abide with Him forever. The more we are transformed into His image while on earth, the more we will understand our relationship with Him in heaven for all eternity. That's why we can now clearly see and understand why it is essential to die to ourselves while we are on earth because that directly impacts our state in heaven.

In the spiritual realm, we need to consider everything we do in the physical. Taking what the Lord is leading us into is not to be taken lightly and is not optional because we must believe that He knows the way and the truth and life (Luk. 14: 26-33). One of the biggest hindrances to do what God tells us to do is the fear of man. The consequence of following the fear of man, the agony of recognizing some closeness to Him is lost because it was not taken seriously, is far beyond fathomable. In understanding more of the long-term consequences of not letting the Lord lead our life, we must realize how careful we have to be by giving heed to His Word.

This is why the devil tries by any mean possible to hold man from following the precepts and orders of the Lord, hindering us from living as close as possible to Him and not leading others to Jesus Christ. In heaven, things are revealed regarding our dos and don'ts, and by this, we come to understand all the opportunities we were exposed to while being here on earth out of having the fear of man. Just thinking about how much we missed out on because of this becomes agonizing for us.

> *And do not be afraid of those who kill the body but cannot kill the soul, but rather be afraid of Him who can destroy both soul and body in hell (Gehenna). (Matthew 10:28)*

Jesus is clearly telling us what we should be afraid of, and simultaneously He is also letting us know of whom we shouldn't be afraid: men and worldly circumstances. Interesting that He is saying "not to fear those who can kill the body" by that, He is pointing directly toward man's great enemy, the fear of man. The fear of man will make us do all the crazy things we never dreamed we would do. If we look back on our life, we can see where the fear of man led us. It often has to do with the fear of being left alone or standing out from the crowd. Through purgation, we come to enter into the fear of the Lord, and it is a trait we grow deeper and deeper into because we grow into becoming more and more desperate of losing Him out of love. The fear of God is the love for God. It is birthed from walking with the Lord. The desperation of losing Him out of love is a necessity we need. Otherwise, we will carry on from the fear of man, and we won't do what God tells us. This implies that we can only do one of the two. The consequence of walking in the fear of man is that we lose our relationship with God, and the consequence is to face the reality of where we end up in eternity.

In the eyes of God, we are more valuable than anything else; He doesn't need us in terms of being complete within Himself, but He loves us and, by this, needs us. In this way, the love becomes free, which is the foremost trait of love: it provides freedom. For God to have an intimate relationship with us and love us all, He gave His only begotten Son for the redemption of restoring the relationship. God proved His love toward us through an action that was the most expensive one He could offer. When we understand how much God loves us, we have found the key to losing the fear of man.

> *Are not two little sparrows sold for a penny? And yet not one of them will fall to the ground without your Father's leave (consent) and notice. But even the very hairs of your head are all numbered. Fear not, then; you are more value than many sparrows. (Matthew 10:29-31)*

There is such a misconception of what it means to do for Him. Agape love is not determined by conditions produced by man's work, to turn up and down the volume of God's love for us. It is unchangeable, ready given by His grace unto all. When the Holy Spirit comes to abide within, He helps us live a worthy, noble, decent, and wonderful life. All the fruits of the Holy Spirit are being outpoured and reflected through us. We become the fruits of the Spirit. That's the whole point. To become the vessel, He will, along the way, ask us to lose certain attitudes and behaviors that don't reflect the fruits of the Spirit (Gal. 5:22-23). And when He is asking us to lose these traits, most often through testing and trials, this involves we are to take a stand for God, and in that, He is purging us from the fear of man.

He knows all the hair on our heads, and they are numbered. When one falls off, God still knows how many are left, and when we grow a new hair, He knows that number too, and He knows this for everyone here on earth (Luk. 12:7). That's love, to care so much for someone so well to know these tiny things. The magnitude of His amour, patience, and strength through love shows how much He cares for all of the affairs and faculties in our lives. Waiting with a strength of patience for us to grow, He has the strength to wait in love for us, yet always forging us because, in love, He longs for us to mature in order to abide closer in Him.

Through this, we are taken by the awe of His love for us that He should care for us in such a small thing, which is such a boundless and vast affair for us to comprehend, and that eventually enables us to love likewise. To know His love for us enables us to trust Him, and thus the fear of man dies. Love cast out fear (1 Joh. 4:18).

God gave His only begotten Son, enabling us to live together, come into a relationship with Him and be coheirs with Christ. Out of God's great passion for us and how God is carrying it out, we can only conclude; that God is in control. Therefore, we have nothing to fear because He exclaims that He knows everything about us, which points directly to the fact that He loves us. We only search out the people we care for, and God is like that with us. Out of this, growth sets in motion for us to want to search Him out more to grasp the depth of His love for us, and the more we search, the more we want it because His love unfolds a deeper relationship with Him, and the reverential fear of the Lord is maturing within us.

> *Therefore, everyone who acknowledges Me before men and confesses Me [out of a state of oneness with Me], I will also acknowledge him before My Father Who is in heaven and confess [that I am abiding in] him. But whoever denies and disowns Me before men, I also will deny and disown him before My Father Who is in heaven. (Matthew 10:32-33)*

We must confess Jesus because that is the open door for Him to go to the Father and intercede on our behalf. In the confession lie the open-door blessings of Him turning our whole life into this beautiful walk of life with Him. One must understand the principle of confession working; hence we know God cannot lie. Then obviously, He cannot go against His own principle because that would be lying. By this, we must spiritually grasp that even though God loves us, by all means, He cannot perform His working in our lives in a life that is not confessed to the Lord.

In all the affairs we undergo in life, the principle of confession to the Lord is always one we need to take; in each situation, we either confess we belong to God or the world. In the carnal man, temptations arise not to confess in Christ but to man and the world. This default in the carnal exists as long we are here on earth because it's its nature. Therefore, we must be keenly aware of confessing that we belong to Christ. The heritage of Jesus

Christ is received through the confession of belonging to Him; we have to say yes to Jesus, and by this exclaiming, He is King, Master, and High Priest. There is a confessing of knowing the other in relationships, and if there is no confession, there is no relationship. We cannot claim the inheritance of Christ if we don't confess we are in a family with Him. When we confess Him, we repress the fear of man because we stop being led emotionally, which often is fear-based.

> *Do not think that I have come to bring peace upon the earth; I have not come to bring peace, but a sword. (Matthew 10:34)*

In the coming of Jesus Christ, the light was brought forth; thus, one could differentiate between light and darkness, which is very obliviously made clear in His presence. When He rose from the dead, His Spirit was poured out for all to be able to choose to walk in the Light and come to terms with the canal man. In choosing His Spirit, Light, war will break out; spiritual powers and principalities will close in (Matt. 4:1-11). This occurrence also occurs in our prayer life; every time the Lord leads us onto more depth of His Spirit, the devil and the carnal will try to hinder us until defeated; all done by us holding on to Jesus. Therefore, we must take heed and search out the warnings He is pointing to so we don't succumb to the temptation of abiding in the fear of man. Satan always moves us into the temptation of staying in the fear of man, that's his nature, and in giving heed to him and not having the fear of the Lord, we will fall into temptation. This takes place in a very subtle and almost unnoticed way.

Interestingly, there is no mention of Adam and Eve loving the Lord in the Bible. They knew the Lord, but there was no fear of losing Him, and so they did (Gen. 3). However, they had it all but lost it all because she gave heed to the wrong perception, and Adam did not protect her as he should have because God told Adam first not to eat the fruit of the forbidden tree (Gen 2:17).

> *For I have come to part asunder a man from his father, and a daughter from her mother, and a newly married wife from her*

*mother-in-law- And a man's foes will be they of his own household. (Matthew 10:35-36)*

His Spirit parts asunder even our dear ones from our lives if they are not aligning up His Spirit. Holding dear means what is closest to our hearts. God is in this matter making that exchange so that He becomes our number one, making Him our dearest one to our heart. We must understand that we cannot recognize what is truly the most precious thing in life because the nature of the carnal man fails to recognize it because the foundation of the carnal man is the fear of man; it is emotionally led. Out of this, we must grasp that it is He making the exchange; the carnal man dies as the Holy Spirit takes over. The nature of man is in no condition to comprehend such refined spiritual affairs; this can only be the working of the Holy Spirit.

When the Holy Spirit takes over, what is shaped within us is communion with Jesus. By this, we perceive that the death of our carnal man is taken over by His Spirit and enables us to endure and handle difficult situations. In our weaknesses, He can work mightily through us (2 Cor.12:9). This scripture comes to life in our lives. Knowing from the Bible what takes place is of utmost importance because the ways of the Lord are so incredibly different from how we move in the world. If we fail to recognize that this is how He is using our weakness, we will try to escape it. A handed-over life to Christ is where everything is given to Him (Luk. 14:27), which is the requirement for even to begin understanding and grasp His ways. Even the handing over of our time because we cannot tell how long a good prayer takes; by this, we see we must lose track of keeping God on a schedule and understand by heart that God works out of time but is moving in time.

When oppression and pressure occur in our relationship with Jesus, we must know the force of the mighty weapon called prayer. We need to be instructed on the importance right away. Otherwise, we easily lose faith, hope, and love because the onslaught begins immediately. When Jesus was baptized, the devil immediately began to tempt Him to try to make Him fall away from His calling. This is also for us to recognize that this is what takes place when Jesus is revealed in our lives. The only resting place we have is spiritually residing in Him. It's the only place where we are at rest, and by this letting Him fight the battles of the dragons and beasts. Simultaneously in this, He is, of course, not only keeping us under His mighty wing but also revealing the secrets of His nature. This occurs especially during battles because this is the only place where we can grasp the deeper meaning of Him, His precepts, and insight in the scripture (Job 43:5). Alongside that, a constant deeper merging occurs, and the circle of these affairs continues.

> *He who loves [and takes more pleasure in] father or mother more than [in] Me is not worthy of Me; and he who loves [and takes more pleasure in] son or daughter more than [in] Me is not worthy of Me; (Matthew 10:37)*

That means the Lord will ask us to live a life that reflects this. In loving our children more than God makes us unworthy, understanding that what He provides for us, giving ourselves away, is so much greater that there is no comparison between these two matters. It is understanding that when we love our children more than God, we will follow our feelings and take our children into consideration first, instead of confiding in the Lord first, as we should in all affairs. This is fear-based living.

The life He offers us is beyond the comprehension of the sweet love between parents and children. This occurs naturally in His presence. We experience this exchange within when we spend time in His presence, when He purges us, removes all the old carnal ways, and then makes the exchange by filling us with His intentions and love, which is true life. The way to fall away from the Lord is by not spending time in His presence and letting worldly affairs take over. The flesh is so fickle, it tends its own ways, and our children are something that can make us lose focus in life and make us stumble in not being careful in handing them over to the Lord. By turning our attention to Him, we are letting God in on all our affairs with our children and are making Him the provider of solutions. We cannot hold onto anything in our lives because it is not ours. Not even our children.

> *And he who does not take up his cross and follow Me [cleave steadfastly to Me, conforming wholly to My example in living and, if need be, in dying also] is not worthy of Me. (Matthew 10:38)*

The passion and love He has for us, displayed on the Cross, is the same passion we grow into. By this, we undergo death and resurrection of life; we die to the old life in being saved into the new life. We are turned over, fully and completely, into the hands of Christ. Jesus took up His Cross, which also shows us, by leading the way, that we must also take up our cross. We need to learn to be convicted and be constantly able to learn and grow in Him and do whatever it takes. In not doing so, we are not worthy of following Him, understanding that what He offers surpasses far beyond all the life issues and struggles. They are no comparison to the goodness He offers (Rom. 8:18). That means if we are not ready to die, being purged in our inner man; will, emotions, knowledge, righteousness, etc., at any moment or pay the cost, then we are not worthy of Him because He holds and is the greatest value of life. The unwillingness to be purged most often has to do with the fear of man.

What Jesus did on The Cross holds the highest of the highest value. Therefore, it deserves the best of us to be excellent before Him. That's how Holy and worthy Jesus God is. This excellency that is needed comes from the Holy Spirit. It is not something we can produce, understanding again that the nature of carnal man cannot come anywhere near to the smallest degree even to comprehend the grandness of His Holiness. There is only one residence of holiness, and that is within Him. Therefore, we grasp that it is by His Spirit that we are being sanctified and transformed; out of that, we can act and do the excellent for Him. Empathizing that when we get to know Jesus as Lord, the dying to self is strangely something we tend to grow into and desire because we know that the life He is providing and leading us into is what truly is life. By this, we realize without Jesus that there was no life at all, mere death. Scripture becomes a reality within us; when Jesus said, I Am the way and the truth and the life (Joh. 14:6), the authenticity of His truth-spoken words is brought to life. We grow more and more into wanting to be purged in order to die, all out of we have tasted what life is. This is the analogy Jesus refers to when He speaks of come and drink for those who are thirsty, referring to someone claiming to know the taste of water but never have had a drink and then gets a drink of water; only by this, we can differentiate between the two.

## Chapter 3: The Importance of Having the Fear of God

*Whoever finds his [lower] life will lose it [the higher life], and whoever loses his [lower] life on My account will find it [the higher Life]. (Matthew 10:39)*

In holding onto and thereby living with all that is included in the lower life, which is led by the fear of man, we will stay there and lose the life Jesus offers: the higher life, the reverential fear of the Lord. However, we receive the higher life by turning our lives toward Jesus and accepting Him as our Savior. Through the revelation in this matter, we come to terms with what is dead cannot give life; that our life was not life at all but merely living stones waiting to come to life (1 Pet. 2:5). The wanting and searching for life is a trademark the Lord has provided within all of mankind, all in order to find Him. What we will gain is real life; we come to understand that we haven't really been living. We realize that the spiritual life needs to be revealed in us to say that we live and have life. We find out that we have been looking for something for our whole life, trying different things to find that release of peace and lose the fear of man. We try to build a life where we are "on top of things" and to stay there. We try to create a life of security to lose the fear of man and to find peace.

In our search, we might dive deeper into work and try to work a way into freedom, unsuccessfully, because, in this way, we only grow in desire. We find more gain is also more responsibility (we can only maintain the riches of life when abiding in Christ. This is the only place where we won't fall for the god of mammon). Maybe we try to find a sense of belonging through a spouse, but that doesn't work either because the spouse cannot fill the gap in the heart. After all, that is reserved for the Holy Spirit. So we build, we do, we work, and we try to find a sense of it all so that we can come to a place where we can rest and live a life absent of the fear of man. We are all looking for something spiritual to lift us up and elevate us into something more so that we can find peace and escape man's fear. Most people can't define what that more is, but there is always this deep searching inside. God has created us like that so that we will search and find Him. He gave us the ability to search, and by this, we must fathom that it is He leading us to Him. He longs for us to search and find Him and then search Him out afterward.

All in all, to know everything that is on His heart and to come into a relationship with Him and seek out His mysteries because they are so marvelous. We can only receive the revelations of all of this when we are in the spiritual realm with Him because His Spirit needs to merge with ours for revelation to be poured out within us.

We go through this process when we say yes to Jesus, which continues in our prayer life. There always has to be a yes to Him for us to grow in Him. We can hinder the process by saying no by doing and wanting our way. This also applies in prayer. However, we must know that He always stands with open arms toward us in His mercy. One can clearly understand the importance of having the reverential fear of the Lord; because in our weak nature, we cannot produce any good. We cannot grasp the depth of love and life which is Jesus. The fear of the Lord is the foundation of our Christian life and must be firmly installed for any spiritual growth to occur.

# Chapter 4

# Hard to Pray

**The difference between carnal and spiritual prayers**

*THEREFORE, [there is] now no condemnation (no adjudging guilty of wrong) for those who are in Christ Jesus, who live [and] walk not after the dictates of the flesh, but after the dictates of the Spirit. For the law of the Spirit of life [which is] in Christ Jesus [the law of our new being] has freed me from the law of sin and of death. For God has done what the law could not do, [its power] being weakened by the flesh [the entire nature of man without the Holy Spirit]. Sending His own Son in the guise of sinful flesh and as an offering for sin, [God] condemned sin in the flesh [subdued, overcame, deprived it of its power over all who accept that sacrifice], So that the righteous and just requirement of the law might be fully met in us who live and move not in the ways of the flesh but in the ways of the Spirit [our lives governed not by the standards and according to the dictates of the flesh, but controlled by the Holy Spirit]. (Romans 8:1-4)*

God overcame the sinful nature of man, eliminating sin and death. The Old Testament way of praying is over. It is finished. That means prayers go unanswered because they are not aligned with the New Covenant prayers or doing things your own way, meaning doing the opposite of what the Lord asks of you. This is obvious, so I will not address this matter in-depth here. However, we must address the Old Testament with respect to the New Testament prayers. God put an end to the Mosaic Law and thus the moral struggle that was fought inside every man before and during the Mosaic Law. He ended Mosaic Law by fulfilling it so that we were no longer subservient to it. Jesus enabled us to live a Holy life by sending the Holy Spirit to abide in those who have accepted and believed in Him. That also includes a prayerfully Holy life through the Holy Spirit abiding within. Prayers in the Old Testament differ from how we should pray according to the New Testament. It is crucially important that we are aware of this difference. The difference between the two is this: in the Old Testament, you have to do or act in a certain way to receive the blessing, as opposed to the New Testament, where we receive the blessing by accepting Jesus as our Lord. Jesus fulfilled the Old Testament Law, and because of that, we can receive the blessings by believing in Jesus Christ. Allow me to expound on the blessing. Blessing is when we enter into a relationship with Jesus Christ and receive a life where we can walk in a close intimate relationship with Him, in both this life and in the life to come. He fulfilled every prayer in the Old Testament, and we can now receive them by believing in Him. He has fulfilled everything we are ever going to need. He contains all prayers, and He is our prayer, which is why we should look at "His face," meaning we come to know Him, to be with Him, and He becomes our best friend and the keeper of our life. And not just look to "His hands," which means we only come to Him when we want something from Him, mostly a physical need.

Let us discuss this. Everything that needs to be restored in our lives was restored 2000 years ago on the Cross. If every need we will ever have is restored on the Cross, then our prayer life is also restored (Col. 1:19-22). This is why when we pray, we cannot use the Old Testament prayers because they are obsolete. Jesus finished The Law of works on The Cross, which includes praying Old Testament prayers that are prayed out of works. Most people in the Old Testament were not people filled with the Holy Spirit. There were some whose prayers were pleasing to God because He had put His hands upon their lives. Jesus fulfilled all works on the Cross, even those we tend to address in prayer through works in the carnal man, mostly by speaking a lot and being strong-willed and emotionally led. The carnal man's nature is to be in charge; therefore, training is required to let go of working in prayer. We achieve this by yielding and waiting for the Lord in prayer. There must be a constant emptying out of ourselves: a constant dying and purgation. This occurrence on the Cross is a picture frame for us to consider every time we change. This rhythm occurs each time. We will, to some degree, experience the dying on the Cross ourselves and thus come to fathom the importance of understanding and contemplating the Cross. And we should strive for this in prayer, to humble ourselves and wait long enough for the flesh to become quiet, thus enabling us to hear and see what occurred on the Cross. Beloved, this takes time. It takes time to deepen in prayer.

We must have faith in the New Covenant prayers and believe in Him in order to receive Him. Also, in our need to heal, we move into thanksgiving towards Him for the healing and restoration on the Cross; we walk with this hope, and we use our faith to receive it: understanding that during prayer, we need to take hold of faith so we can deepen into prayer. By holding on to faith in prayer, we receive answered prayers. And in that, we find the difference between these two covenant prayers.

This is why it becomes hard to pray if the Old Testament prayers and the New Testament prayers are mixed. Frustration will arise because one's prayers go unanswered. If we go to another country and try to live according to our nation's laws, we can easily end up in trouble. Many people practice this in their prayer life: bringing their own set of prayer rules into the nation of God where we are to follow other laws. This will never work. He has His set of Laws, and if we are to receive His heritage, we need to apply the Laws of the New Covenant prayers to our lives. The main precept of God is to believe in Christ Jesus and the completed work of the Cross. The Cross is somehow always involved in our prayer. As one can clearly see, we need to go to Jesus in our prayer closet; we yield to Him, recognizing what He has done for us. We move into thanksgiving in our prayer time.

We recognize and understand in our hearts that every provision is taken care of, and that is what we thank Him for in our prayer time. This is why we come to the point of deep recognition of how much we need Him in all areas of our lives. We must recognize that our carnal man is dead; the old life is over. The Old Testament prayers come from a lifestyle of works. That means they are brought forth by following, doing right: then one receives a blessing, whereas in doing wrong, only condemnation is left. This is what

Jesus accomplished so that we no longer need to work our way into a righteous prayer. Nobody could ever do this right, and this is what Jesus came down to show us. In the Old Testament, this was the main point for all to agree that we need a Saviour. The people who were anointed in the Old Testament and prayed rightfully did so because the Lord had anointed them beforehand. In the Old Testament, the Lord was still the one authorizing the rightful prayers because He was the one who had anointed them and thus enabled them to pray rightfully. The Bible tells us that we don't know how to pray as we should. After the Cross, Jesus did not only change the prayer life. He also enabled everyone to pray pleasingly to God. Now everybody is invited to the table. The Holy Spirit filled the people, and they are moved to pray; His Spirit enables us. Therefore, we move into yielding, waiting, and thanksgiving because we fathom all the completed work on The Cross for each step.

In the New Testament prayers, we can still find the "help-us" prayers, but they come from the knowledge of the heart of God. This is too great a problem for us, so we ask for help in faith. We are moved forth by knowing that we can't alter the situation, but we know He can. This becomes a prayer of faith. And this is the trademark of the New Testament. The Old Testament prayers come forth through a hope of Him answering if we have acted according to His Law, but no faith abides in that: merely addressing the matter of works in prayer, as opposed to abiding in faith.

Some examples of the difference between these two covenant prayers - Old Testament prayers versus New Testament prayers are:

- Where shall I go? As opposed to, thank You for leading my steps; I trust You.
- What shall I say? As opposed to, thank You for putting your words into my mouth.
- What shall I do? As opposed to, thank You for leading and guiding my every step.

When we pray Old Testament prayers, we are not in alignment with what Jesus did on the Cross. Yet, in the sovereignty of our Lord Jesus, we should know that there is still love for us even though we are doing it wrong. He displays this for us through the convictions of how and where we are wrong, without condemnation.

However, before discovering we are praying Old Testament prayers, spiritual inner fatigue arises. Desiccation, fatigue, irritation, and desperation, and in all of these feelings life stands still with no sign of movement of the Lord in our lives. There is no sign of the fruits of the Holy Spirit. Because of this, we can see that a long period of time may pass before discovering why our prayers are lifeless. The Old Testament prayers He has already fulfilled through the Cross. He wants us to come in and receive the heritage He has provided for us. We do this through yielding, waiting, and worshiping Him and with the full assurance that He is taking care of the circumstances and situations in our lives.

Not to misinterpret the fact that we are doers of the Word; there are always things He is asking us to do. We wait in prayer just as we must learn to wait in the physical world. We yield in prayer and keep following the prescription the Lord has given us for doing in our lives, which is often repetitive. We worship Him and express our thanksgiving and gratitude for our life. The best prescription for combatting our enemy is to turn our eyes to His face. An arduous and strenuous prayer life arises from failing to take the time to yield to and wait for the Lord. This is experienced as a physical and mental hardship and fatigue, where it seems you are getting nowhere in prayer. You must walk through the desert to come to the water, wait, and yield. One can understand more through the heart by reading about the purgation and inner transformation of deep prayer life. But reading about it should never be a substitute for spending time with the Lord Jesus. Hence He is the redeemer of it all, which means the mysteries of Christ are only revealed in Him.

*Elena Radef*

# Chapter 5

# The Impact of Words

**Words either bring life or death, likewise in our prayer**

We have to understand the importance of the choice of words we speak because they directly affect our lives and everything that happens in our circumstances. We are the ones with that influence; we can influence circumstances with words. Jesus needed only to speak one or a few words for the situation He was in to change. He fully recognized who He was; recognized the authority He carried, what His mission here on earth was, and how to operate in the spirit. So that when He spoke, the Words executed these means. All of that we have inherited through Him. He made all of that possible on the Cross.

To do as He did, we need to constantly be in fellowship with Him and give heed to He leadership. This is the way Jesus prescribed for us to walk. That was how He walked with the Father; He displayed the pattern for us to take hold of. The Words in the Bible are alive, living, and breathing, and they will stand forever because God is the Word.

*In the beginning [before all time] was the Word (Christ), and the Word was with God, and the Word was God Himself. (John 1:1)*

The revelation of the power of the Word comes through the Holy Spirit. There is no other way; it must come directly from the source itself. We can never claim to be the ones that "get it" or "understood" it by intellect by reading about it. The only way for us is through the Holy Spirit.

We have many great theologians with many theories claiming to know the Bible, quoting many scriptures. Still, without the Holy Spirit, it will never be alive. That means we don't have the fruits of the Spirit in action: signs, wonders, and miracles, and the Bible can never be in any way understood revelatory unless the person reading it is a Holy Spirit-filled person.

> *He who comes from above (heaven) is [far] above all [others]; he who comes from the earth belongs to the earth, and talks the language of earth [his words are from an earthly standpoint]. He Who comes from heaven is [far] above all others [far superior to all others in prominence and in excellence]. (John 3:31)*

Considering all of this, we can see how "careful" we must be when we are in prayer. We can't afford to pray carnal, vain, talkative prayers because they will have no effect, and we end up frustrated, dry, tired, and at unease.

Knowing Him whilst being here on earth directly affects our life in eternity. Understanding the affairs of the order, precepts, and statues of our Lord provides the right prescription for us to fathom what we need to be doing while being here on earth, and that will bring us into a close relationship with Him in heaven without any remorse or regret of things we know we should have done on earth. We will still learn in heaven, but for us to choose Him here on earth, unseen for the human eye to recognize Him and not understand Him, brings great pleasure to Him (Matt. 5:3). By this, we honor Him. The reward in heaven is the close relationship with Him, abiding in His presence forever.

Therefore, our prayer life should consist of us searching Him out in order to know what He wants us to do in every moment in life, taking into consideration the affairs of the afterlife. When we are praying Holy Spirit prayers, we are not just praying for life at the moment, but we are most certainly praying for the lost souls as well (Luk. 19:10, 2 Pet. 3:9). Who else but the Holy Spirit-filled people could pray with efficiency for them, none! Therefore, this should be one of our main topics in prayer. So, if we just sit in our own carnal prayers pronouncing words hereof, the only thing that is being produced is vain prayers and wasted time. This the devil is very aware of, so he keeps us busy with the affairs of life for us not to understand the importance of praying Holy Spirit prayers that changes the spiritual atmosphere and draw in the lost souls. Holy Spirit-filled prayers involve tongue-speaking prayers that move the Spirit into a place where the utterance of words can take place. So that the words that flow derive from the Holy Spirit. Often, this requires mainly tongue-speaking prayers for a good period of time before the utterance of words comes. And sometimes, no words appear, but the tongues-speaking prayers become more intense. There is, therefore, no fact list to how the Spirit is moving (Joh. 3:8).

We must come to a point in our walk with Christ where we know that the Lord knows all of our needs - when, how, and where to fulfill them and that He does—fulfilling the ones that have derived from the fleshly spiritual heart, His heart, and desire for us. For this reason, we should pay attention to not using our time pronouncing carnal dead prayers, which just steal our precious time from Him. When the Holy Spirit is flowing through us in prayer, the river of His Words will automatically start to flow through us. We don't have to invent useful prayers. Instead, we must focus on emptying ourselves for Him to flow through us. We cannot pray as we ought, the Bible tells us. This must come to our remembrance. When the Holy Spirit prays through us, righteous prayers are being poured out for situations we would know very little of at the right moment in time. By this, we see that we are merely a vessel, and that is our purpose in being such because, in this, we are of most use to Him (2 Cor. 12:9). A vessel will always and only be a vessel. It must come to terms with what it is created for; only then can it be of any use.

> *Again He said to me, Prophesy to these bones and say to them, O you dry bones, hear the word of the Lord. Thus says the Lord God to these bones: Behold, I will cause breath and spirit to enter you, and you shall live; (Ezekiel 37:4-5)*

What was dead will come to life, and strongholds that kept us as prisoners are broken when we speak His Word. We can clearly see, in prayer and life, that we need to learn to talk His language. If I go to China and want to live there and nobody talks my language, it will be no good to keep talking my language. I have to learn their language. Otherwise, it will cause me much frustration on many levels in life. It is the same situation with God. It is us that need to change to adapt and understand His ways.

*For the Word that God speaks is alive and full of power (making it active, operative, energizing, and effective); it is sharper than any two-edged sword, penetrating to the dividing line of the breath of life (soul) and [the immortal] spirit, (Hebrew 4:12)*

God's Word is sharp. It cuts through everything; it separates the carnal man from Spirit-filled man, and because of that, we can see our will compared to God's will for our lives. The Word of the Lord is revelatory; it reveals the difference, teaching us the difference because we are ourselves unable to figure it out. God molds us into His likeness to lead us in every aspect of life, of how to live a righteous life before Him.

The same process happens in our prayer life; His Word comes and separates us from our carnal nature and lifts us up in a revelatory way. By that, we get to comprehend and understand that the supernatural becomes natural in our prayer life and how it is connected with the physical life.

That's why when we worship and sing the Word of the Lord, He responds. He is spiritually lifting us up, separating us from our deepest anxieties, the rebellion of the will, pride, perverse, lustful nature, ignorance, fear, etc. The rapture of people we see is displayed on different occasions in the Bible (Gen. 5:24, Acts 8:39, Heb.11:5). John described this occurrence when the angel spoke to John, "to come up here" in the book of Revelation (Joh. 1:10, 4:1). The occurrence takes place in devoted prayer; we are being lifted up in rapture. It splits the line between the carnal, soul, and spirit, and we get to live in the freedom of Christ. Scripture should, by all means, come to life within us.

*and of joints and marrow, (Hebrew 4:12)*

It cuts right into the deepest core of a human body and soul, right into that which needs to be cut off. It points to everything inside of us, and nothing is hidden. It comes under God's magnifying glass. Everything is exposed - every sinful nature of ours and every attitude that is not right. Everything that is binding us, everything that does not align with the Word of the Lord. In His grace and mercy, He points to them one at a time. He separates us from every stronghold, everything that hinders us from walking in more freedom in Him. The moment He is pointing them out, that is where the anointing is upon the situation for us to take hold of it.

Let us elaborate on the sanctification process we undergo with Christ with our souls.

When saying yes to Him in our conversion, the Holy Spirit comes to abide within us. The minute that happened, every part of the old nature was uninstalled, and the new creation was installed. A major shift took place. When something is uninstalled, it is no longer in operation; that means that those sets of rules and orders are no longer in law. They are obsolete. Therefore, we have to grab hold of the new laws and rules that came with the Holy Spirit by obeying them.

The Holy Spirit abides as a complete Spirit within us. Therefore, we can say the old is dead, but we still have to use our will to set the new law of the Holy Spirit in function by using our will to do what He tells us. This occurs when the Holy Spirit is being purged through our whole being, and His will and our will become one—cleansing our soul.

Sometimes what the Lord carries us through, sanctifying us, might move fast, and other times it's over a long period of time. For this reason, in some areas where we were hurt extensively and therefore require time to restore, we need to be thoroughly purged so that we can stand in our calling. The areas where we are being thoroughly cleansed most often have to do with our calling. However, it is a quick process at other times because there are very few or no wounds on the soul to restore.

This is intertwined with what purpose He wants to use the gifting within us. Whether fast or longsome, all purgation is all based upon where He will place us. There is also the sanctification process or purgation we undergo in the spiritual, but that is a different matter. I am only addressing the sanctification or purgation process concerning the soul's nature. Although some parts overlap each other.

> *[of the deepest parts of our nature], exposing and sifting and analyzing and judging the very thoughts and purposes of the heart. (Hebrew 4:12)*

When our soul is being cut off from the carnal, and we are spiritually being lifted up, we can easily discern right from wrong. Conviction becomes very clear because His presence brings forth the revelatory kingdom of Christ. We are no longer bound by our emotions, will, and mind - the soulish nature. All of His ways become at hand for us.

> *For now we are looking in a mirror that gives only a dim (blurred) reflection [of reality as in a riddle or enigma], but then [when perfection comes] we shall see in reality and face to face! Now I know in part [imperfectly], but then I shall know and understand fully and clearly, even in the same manner as I have been fully and clearly known and understood [by God]. 1 (Corinthians 13:12)*

When we are in front of a mirror that is reflecting Jesus, it is very clear to see what is not reflecting Jesus on our faces. When we are looking at the life of Jesus, it is very clear to see where our life is not reflecting Jesus'. When we come close to His Holiness, it becomes very clear for us, within an instant, where our life is not reflecting the Holy Spirit in quality and the nature of Christ. In this manner, the Holy Spirit brings conviction to us. In the deep spiritual yielded prayer, the inner transformation occurs. The knowledge of what is on the mind and heart of God comes without wording. It is a spiritual knowledge revealed. The mere presence of the Holy Spirit brings forth the conviction needed for repentance to take place. Repentance is a necessity, a requirement for us to grow in spiritual maturity. Without it, we cannot grow. When conviction is brought forth, we clearly see where we have failed, and with ease, we ask for forgiveness, and repentance can occur. The Holy Spirit performs the freedom of asking for forgiveness. It is not something we can do either because we cannot perform the workings of the Holy Spirit. We cannot pray as we ought (Rom. 8:26). We are merely a vessel, making ourselves available for the Holy Spirit to pour Himself through. This is the only road to restoration and for us to come and abide in His presence. God is always ministering to us, leading us on to the path of His righteous living so that we will come to love Him, and when we do, we bring glory to His name.

He is all the traits of an amazing life.

# Chapter 6

# Understanding Humility

**The difference between true and false humility**

We have to stay fresh in our humility. That means that we can't go back and use the old things that made us humble, needless to say, because we also have to grow in our humility. We have to grow from one level of humility to another because we go from glory to glory. These two are aligned together. When we grow in humility, we grow in glory. We increase in both areas simultaneously; we grow in humility in our sanctification. Therefore, it is important to understand the principle of growth in our humility. Otherwise, we could very easily miss the workings of growing in humility.

Most of us grow in humility through difficult times. In moving through those valleys of the shadow of death, we can't turn back to those old spiritual dwelling places and think we grow deeper in our humility in that one area. We need to be touched on new aspects of ourselves to grow in humility. Suppose we only lean in on the previous difficult situation, living as if we don't need to grow deeper. In that case, we won't grow, and it becomes a false humility because we think we are finished. This matter is very subtle, and it is not a conscious act of the mind. It's merely outlived unknowingly through the carnal. What happens then is instead of growing deeper in our humility, we become more and more superficial because we think we're doing so well. In other words, there is too much leaning in on the comfort in the carnal. We can never trust the carnal.

The purging from our Lord needs somehow always to be there. Otherwise, the pride of the flesh takes over. The nature of the flesh thinks it is doing well, and by leaning on that inner statement, it will return to its nature: pride and ego. So it constantly needs to be under the guidance of being purged. False humility will boost our ego and pride because people will compliment us on the wrong things; "Oh, you're so humble in giving up yourself by not having any needs." And the ego thrives in this instead of diminishing; pride grows instead of humility, and it grows into false humility—all something the devil uses to keep the person in bondage.

To grow in our sanctification, we must look at and turn to become more and more humble. First, we must become small, so He can grow and increase in us. This is the analogy we must take hold of in our prayer life. The sanctification process starts in our prayer life after our conversion. Then, in our communion with the Lord, He reveals the next step for us to stay humble. He doesn't just pour things on us, unknowingly, but very intentionally. He does this so that we can become mature Christians that can endure spiritual wars and overcome them all to take territory back, increase the population in heaven, and see the freedom of salvation in people's lives while being on earth - all to glorify Him here and beyond. Humility is required in all of these areas.

*He must increase, but I must decrease. [He must grow more prominent; I must grow less so.] (John 3:30)*

The story about the rich man that is asking Jesus how to inherit eternal life is another story that tells us what must be carnally circumcised in our prayer life. It tells us how to do it (Mark. 10).

The story also depicts false humility because the rich young ruler exclaims that he has held all the commandments that Jesus is listing before him. False humility always thinks it got the point or knows the ways of the Lord. The preconceived thinking is false humility. When we are preconceived, we are spiritually closed to the affairs of the Lord and His precepts.

It was difficult for the man to let go of the world's riches. He held on to his possessions because He lacked obedience and humility. It requires humility to hear what Christ is speaking to our hearts.

*And as He was setting out on His journey, a man ran up and knelt before Him and asked Him, Teacher, [You are essentially and perfectly morally] good, what must I do to inherit eternal life [that is, to partake of eternal salvation in the Messiah's kingdom]? And Jesus said to him, Why do you call Me [essentially and perfectly morally] good? There is no one [essentially and perfectly morally] good – except God alone. You know the commandments: Do not kill, do not commit adultery, do not steal, do not bear false witness, do not defraud, honor your father and mother. And he replied to Him, Teacher, I have carefully guarded and observed all these and taken care not to violate them from my boyhood. And Jesus, looking upon him, loved him, and He said to him, You lack one thing; go and sell all you have and give [the money] to the poor, and you will have treasure in heaven; and come [and] accompany Me [walking the same road that I walk]. At that saying the man's countenance fell and was gloomy, and he went away grieved and sorrowing, for he was holding great possessions. (Mark 10:17-22)*

If we hold on to our emotions and riches in prayer, we can't come near and enter into the kingdom of God. Suppose our kingdom, our life, emotions, thinking, style, and so on are more important than God's. In that case, we can't come near His kingdom because that is idolatry in the eyes of the Lord.

Here we perceive the way that is comfortable to the flesh does not bring us in alignment with the precepts and statues of our Lord. On the contrary, we move further away from the intimate relationship with Him. By holding on to the conformity of the carnal, we will eventually make a picture and phantasy about how God is, and the reality of Him and His nature disappears. Along the way, we will eventually get more and more frustrated and in deep distress. It will always be an unclear sight of God in perceiving Him, even in the smallest means, through our emotions, when in doing so, we make Him into something which He is not. Another serious matter in this way of approaching the Lord is that we move into the consideration that we are at the same level as God because we think we understand God.

Notice the scripture says that Jesus loved him. So even in our wrong way of perceiving the affairs, He is leading us by correction because He loves us. That is very important to remember when we make mistakes, and He is correcting us; the Lord does not lose His love for us. However, He can't lead us on the right path and fill the position in our hearts. He points to what is hidden in our hearts, and we must, when He does, repent and turn to Him in all our affairs. This is the obedient heart He is looking for no matter how difficult the issue. There has to be a constant willingness to hand over our affairs, humble ourselves by handing them over to Him, and die to ourselves when He points to a questionable trade within us. By this, He is telling us where we need to change.

Change of the old life comes along when we say yes to the steps. He is asking us to take in our purgation. This is the process of dying to self to become humble, understanding that we have to be willing to let go of the old life security net before we can receive the new life, He has in store for us. The security net is patterns and ways we perceive, understand, and live our life. That must die in the remembrance of we are a new creation; that means our life will become new in all ways and affairs. Humbleness grows in the uncertainty of not being able to lean in on old patterns. This is the faith walk He asks us to step into in all our affairs.

What God does in prayer is that He is changing us bit by bit, erasing old emotions, ways of thinking, and knowledge, and filling us with His. He is putting to death the old man, removing pride and unfolding the new creation within us, installing humbleness. The old ways and emotions die within, we change, we start to think anew, and we do and act differently. Die means that it won't come to life again. The only thing that remains the same is the body's outer appearance. Everything else changes. That is the purgation we undergo in the arms of Christ. Therefore, we must decrease, as John talks about. We must nullify and make our hearts still to hear God and sense any leadership from Him in our lives. We must lose the fatness of our lifestyle in prayer, pride, and ego, and only then can we begin to see and hear Him. The first place for it to change is in the spiritual. Afterward, we will see it manifest in the physical. This is the order of the precepts and statutes of God. To lose our opinion and the fatness is not something we can alter within ourselves. It happens as a natural consequence of spending time with Him.

## Chapter 6: Understanding Humility

We have to become so small in prayer that we can enter into the kingdom of God. Humble and low, free from any thoughts and opinions about what will happen in prayer. That's why Jesus suddenly talked about how it is easier for a camel to go through the eye of a needle. We have to become very, very small. This part on our behalf requires time in the waiting on God. We come low. We diminish ourselves, and we keep moving back to ground zero in our hearts. We train our minds to keep coming back into His presence in our hearts. We pray with an inner listening ear, pray in tongues, become quiet, wait, and don't ask questions because we don't want to. Humble and waiting. The waiting part is not dependent on time. It moves out of time; therefore, the waiting can be a move within a few minutes, or it can take hours. In both scenarios, we lose track of time. The focus is not on time, so it doesn't matter if it takes a long time, in the physical or not. His presence is so glorious; it enables us to forget ourselves and the involvement of time because His Spirit moves out of time and overtakes us.

The only possibility we have that enables us is through the ways and precepts of the Lord. In (Mrk. 10:25), Jesus answers us that all spiritual work is only possible through God. Coming through the needle's eye by losing ourselves, diminishing our carnal nature, is only possible if God takes over and does it through us. We have to become so small and humble from the revelation of how impossible everything is without God.

> *It is easier for a camel to go through the eye of a needle than for a rich man to enter the kingdom of God. And they were shocked and exceedingly astonished, and said to Him and to one another, Then who can be saved? Jesus glanced around at them and said, With men [it is] impossible, but not with God; for all things are possible with God. (Mark 10:25-27)*

Even the taking "over part" is something we have to wait on God to do. The thing we have to do is to wait on God. We can't force Him to come. We can't command anything of Him. We can't force Him to unfold the deeper nature of Him to us. Instead, we must come to a position in prayer where we wait and humble ourselves in the heart toward Him. Only He knows when and where we are at that point in our lives when we can receive the deeper unveiling part of Him. This should be a key position for us in prayer.

We must never take Him for granted even though Jesus Himself says I will never leave you nor forsake you. He is always there, but we cannot take Him for granted. If we only take Him for granted, our walk turns into hyper-grace. Then suddenly, our walk turns into; I can do anything I want; Jesus will never leave me. Neither should we do things out of fear of losing Him all the time. It is also pride because it's the carnal man's interpretation of losing Him, and when it's from the carnal, it can only come forth through pride. It is obviously not something we want to do when we read this. However, in many people's lives, this is happening regularly. It is, though, wrapped up in a subtle way, and by this, it can therefore be tough to detect. We have to be very careful not to let this tendency enter our lives because it can easily enter.

There is a different way of understanding these two elements. When God has purged us, we come to abide in these elements through the perception of the Holy Spirit. In this, we come to have the reverential fear of losing God, and we are abiding in His bosom, knowing that He is there as our Father who will never leave us. These two elements are birthed in the purgation from God's love; therefore, we now perceive these elements correctly.

The difference between these two elements sounds like the following:

| **The carnal** | **The Spiritual** |
| --- | --- |
| I can do whatever I want. | You are my Father, and I love you |
| Hyper grace | Rest in the Lord |
| I am so afraid to lose you, I must do better and work harder. | I love you because you loved me first; I would want to do the things You ask of me |
| Fear of man | Reverential fear of the Lord. |

We must understand that when we spend time with Him, the topic of taking Him for granted becomes a scarcely frightening thing for us because we come to love Him dearly and deeply. So, the possibility for the occurrence of taking Him for granted steps aside. This is because we are so keen on not letting it happen, and that is because of the depth of the love that grows in our hearts; it keeps us on the right path. We clearly see how it is connected to staying low and humble of heart because, in that, we have a spiritual attentive ear and heart.

In returning to the scripture with the rich man, and we reread it, we can see he came to Jesus with this inner attitude of taking Him for granted because later in the text, it says his countenance fell and became gloomy. That's because he for sure thought that he had done all the right things and that he had everything in order. He was not open, humble to what the Lord would answer. He had prefixed ideas about the answer Jesus would bring. The mood only descends when Jesus confronts the carnal, but when we know Jesus in our hearts, we will respond with a: "Yes, Lord" because we know He is right. We know in our hearts He is right because our inner witness bears witness to the Word of the Lord. We can recognize if we are taking Him for granted when we only want Him to bring order in our life so that we can continue in the same manner as before the problem. We come to see that this is not a surrendered life to Jesus, but like the rich man, we want something that is a hindrance for us now to be taken care of, all for us to move on. We are not interested in a deeper inner change; we only want an outer change. Essentially, then our heart's position is not right. Jesus longs for and wants to set things right in our lives, but not how we think. The carnal man's nature doesn't understand His ways and, therefore, will not understand Him (Rom. 11:33). Obedience and humbleness enter the process when we don't have prefixed ideas about the faith walk, and out of that grows the partnership with Jesus (2 Cor. 5:7); He leads, we obey. We come to understand that His ways are higher and better than ours and are in absolutely no comparison. As one can clearly see, there is no room for the attitude of taking Him for granted; the humbleness of heart is lost and it only hinders and delays in every means and matter. Jesus knew the rich man had this attitude because He rebukes him when he calls Him good. Jesus responds to this by saying there is only one perfect and good God. When we only look at Jesus' hands and what He can do for us, we will lose track of Him. That was the rich man's attitude in his heart, and Jesus knew that. Even if we come with this attitude of taking Him for granted and that we just want Him to do a certain thing for us, He still loves us, but like with the rich man, Jesus will point to our weakness for us to become free.

It is important to constantly keep in mind and know that Jesus loves us despite all of our faults. If we don't know this, we will start to think of Him as a condemning and judging God. God is first and foremost the true and perfect expression of love. He will correct us when we are off track like the rich man. There has to be the reverence of fear of the Lord, knowing that He is God, yet at the same time the sweetness and kindness of someone you know intimately, knowing that we are sons and daughters. We have an Abba Father that has made us heirs of all His riches through Christ. These two should co-exist in us at the same time. As seen through the scriptures that we've discussed, our pride most certainly has to die for us to come close to the humbleness that is required to hear and walk in the footsteps of Christ.

# Chapter 7

# Understanding God is our Refuge

**The necessity of God sustaining us in prayer**

Taking refuge in Christ in our prayer life has a lot to do with what prayer is because we can't make it without Christ Jesus. We urgently need to understand this fact. The Bible often and repeatedly talks about how God is our refuge, shield, protector, and cover, and He overshadows us. These are all different ways where God is displaying His character toward us during different circumstances. They all portray different meanings regarding the different situations we are moving along or through.

One person in the Bible who often references God in this matter is David. Because of all that he went through, he needed to experience God in these different ways, all for later purposes, to fulfill God's task, which was to become and be a king. He needed the knowledge of the protection to be able to stand in that calling. We all know what he went through to become king and his living conditions during his time with Saul. David is also the picture for us to reference how we often only have God to lean on during difficult times and that He will come through for us. Let's look at what David is saying and praying in his heart when he sought the Lord for help and encouragement to move on. He is an excellent writer for the revelatory part regarding prayer. He most eloquently tells us the steps in prayer, and by his wording, he tells us what is important to focus on in prayer. Even though he was alone for years in the field with the sheep and had no one to talk to, notice how God sees and knows of every circumstance we go through.

> *For God alone my soul waits in silence; from Him comes my salvation. (Psalm 62:1)*

David talks about how his soul is waiting for God in silence. Notice that David a lot of times says: "my soul." He uses a different language because he is moving on the inner with a clear revelation of how prayer works, knowing what he needs to cast down and what he needs to lift up.

We already see a vital principle at stake, which is waiting patiently on God. David is talking to the emotions within himself that are working against the waiting, which wants to move and take over. The waiting kills the nature of the carnal man. David is positioning himself to wait, knowing that waiting is the salvation of the situation. That is all he is doing within, waiting on God to take Him out, out of the knowledge that he couldn't do it himself. He knows how inadequate he is. So he stayed and waited on the Lord.

In this position, we don't just let our minds wander off, taking a trip on its own. No, we make it submit to the waiting by declaring as David did; soul, be quiet. All sprung from the revelation that through the Holy Spirit, we can express the Words, knowing that it is the power of the Holy Spirit doing the work, casting the carnal man down.

We don't let our emotions steer the time because the carnality will always try to escape it; it is enmity to God; they are antagonistic. Paul also talks about the enmity between emotions and God (Gal. 5:17). It is a matter that we must not take lightly because then our feet will slip in prayer. No, again, we make the emotions submit through waiting. Waiting is the medicine and the cure for carnality's imperfections.

> *For the desires of the flesh are opposed to the [Holy] Spirit, and the [desires of the] Spirit are opposed to the flesh (godless human nature); for these are antagonistic to each other [continually withstanding and in conflict with each other], so that you are not free but are prevented from doing what you desire to do. (Galatians 5:17)*

We must reach a point on the inner, in a revelatory way, that everything comes from Jesus and that He is the door we must walk through in everything in our life. We can do nothing without God. Bearing this in mind and heart brings a whole new fearful depth into prayer that we must, by all means, constantly pursue. Salvation in this context with David means that God is the one taking us out of every burdensome situation. We need to come to this point in prayer where this is outlived in our lives, that everything we do and say comes from this fact; without You, Lord, we can do nothing.

> *He only is my Rock and my Salvation, my Defense and my Fortress, I shall not be greatly moved. (Psalm 62:2)*

In times of trouble and great distress, we tend to lose control and become greatly moved. Only by His Spirit, we won't lose control but have self-control in troublesome times. Without Him, we cannot move through difficult times without becoming greatly moved. We all know how much strength that requires, and we always come short of this. We can become so greatly moved that we lose all sanity. The story of Jesus and the demon-possessed man proved this point (Mrk. 5:1-20). However, during these trials we go through with Christ, we mature into the knowledge of Him keeping us and taking us through every valley of the shadow of death. Therefore, through Him, we can stand.

Out of that, we might experience being hit by circumstances in life and get shaken, but we will not be greatly moved. We will stand firm and not lose our mind or ground; instead, we will see in the spirit what is coming against us. We can then cast it out and command it to leave and, by that, see the glorious hand of God working in our lives. Here we start to exercise the authority of God.

> *How long will you set upon a man that you may slay him, all of you, like a leaning wall, like a tottering fence? (Psalm 62:3)*

David addresses the enemies working against him, asking how long will this continue. David is referring to the tottering fence as him being weak and vulnerable. A fence is something that stands there, no matter the circumstances of the weather. Comparing himself to a tottering fence shows that he knew there was nothing he could do about the situation. In other words, he knew he needed God to take him out. David was left to trust God in the situation. That's the position God often places us in; to wait and to trust solemnly in Him.

> *They only consult to cast him down from his height [to dishonor him]; they delight in lies. They bless with their mouths, but they curse inwardly. (Psalm 62:4)*

We have to be so aware of how we live our lives; whom we confide in – David is talking about people who do one thing and then carry another agenda in their hearts. The people he is addressing are the ones that were after him.

They speak one thing but carry out another thing, also called hypocrites. A lot of times, people are hypocritical out of fear. It starts as a tiny seed of fear but unfortunately if we don't deal with it, it grows into more and more evilness. That is why we have to be careful. It is an eroding position, so we must take out the wrongdoing and thinking when it is small and seemingly weak in our soul. In other words, stopping and redirecting a small stream of water is easier than a river.

We can easily be influenced by what we surround ourselves with and start doing the same slowly but surely. The minute we think that we will never do that, we have fallen spiritually asleep and lost. David is talking about the people who were after him, but in prayer, we have to watch ourselves because the flesh is weak. The flesh is an enmity to God; it wants its way, so we must be cautious. By this, David also displays for us that our confidence is in Christ, not in the carnal man. He is the ever-unchanging confider and the one that will never leave us but always helps us. The carnal will not always help us because it is ever-changing in opinions, moods, feelings, etc. It will surely make us fall at some point. So, when assaults strike against our lives, God leads us to dive deeper into His presence. That is what David did because that was the only option he was left with.

And then he says:

> *Selah [pause, and calmly think of that]! (Psalm 62:4)*

We have to reflect on these things and stress not to engage with people who carry the interest in serving the carnal man. That is what the Pharisees did. That will always hinder or slow us down, eventually carrying us away from God. These people will always appeal to the carnal, the lower life.

It is a process to be led astray. Therefore it requires us to take cautious steps in all matters and affairs, first and foremost in our prayer life. Here we must attend to the need to look out for not creating an image of Jesus through an interpretation in the flesh. The flesh always reasons itself through words and inner discussions. Contrary to what we receive from the Lord, it rests in our inner man in a peaceful way that surpasses our understanding. There is always an abiding peace when He speaks. The Holy Spirit always appeals to our spirit, the higher life.

The inner searching of contemplating our actions and our life is an inner search and quest that must always be ready at hand because we come more and more to fathom the absolute fickleness of the carnal. The ease for the flesh to fall into all kinds of temptations is very nearby, like a shadow that follows around. This is also how the Lord trains us to become spiritually awake so we don't fall into temptations. Through this cautiousness, we become like a sharp sword, discerning the voice of our Lord. Through the inner subtle, attentive care, we become aware of which areas we need to change in our lives.

> *My soul, wait only upon God and silently submit to Him; for my hope and expectation are from Him. (Psalm 62:5)*

Our soul is our will, emotions, and mind. These faculties are moved into a position through the Holy Spirit, enabling and strengthening us to become quiet and submissive. Only through the purgation are we enabled to steer the reins of our soul; coming to fathom it is not us doing it but the Holy Spirit. We come to recognize that there is only one way of asking our Lord for help in prayer, and that is through the mere and total recognition that we are just a vessel. We recognize the requirement of a complete need on Him to walk in our calling. We have no problem with submission when we see that we are a vessel. Patience, courage, and strength are required to mature spiritually, understanding that it is not us that produce these qualities within, but that we must wait for them to mature alongside in the purgation. We are fickle and can't handle very much at a time. We are dearly confronted with our true nature and dearly confronted with His nature. If the process goes too fast, any person can fall away from God because the carnal is weak. Grasping the reality that we cannot discern anything is a foundation that must be laid within us. Then the place of submission becomes our shield and home.

*He only is my Rock and my Salvation; He is my Defense and my Fortress, I shall not be moved. (Psalm 62:6)*

Notice how David stresses out how he knows for sure that it is God who is his fortress and that it has nothing to do with him. He understands that everything revolves around the fact that only God can protect him. David does not take credit for anything because he knows through the situations that God has carried him out of, it was something he absolutely could not do himself. In God, our hope for glory and salvation lies.

*With God rests my salvation and my glory; He is my Rock of unyielding strength and impenetrable hardness, and my refuge is in God! (Psalm 62:7)*

When we are resting in this place with God, nothing can enter that is not from God. He is our impenetrable shield; nothing can harm us. One trait that grows out of experiencing Him being our impenetrable shield is a deep hunger for Him. Over time, we have come to recognize how much He is interfering just at the right moments in our lives. By this, we experience His love for us, over and over. Out of this pattern increases His love within us, and because of that, we lean our whole life upon Him. We now experience the increase of hunger for Him and, by this, for the affairs that are on His heart. One major area that increases within our hearts is salvation; salvation in our lives in all areas as David is describing but also salvation for mankind.

The affairs of time in this matter are of most importance. Pay attention to what David talks about 'with God rests my salvation. There is a matter to consider here; letting our salvation be worked out in God's timing. By this, we are giving Him all our time without any limits.

David shows us the secret hiding place in his Psalms: the intimate prayer life. One can only come to understand it in a revelatory way by experiencing it in one's own prayer life. Therefore, some passages won't make any sense, and one doesn't understand the language of the Psalms if not revealed. Something else David is pointing out is that there seemingly exists a correlation between worship and prayer; they go hand in hand. One cannot function without the other. In displaying this matter, we repeatedly see a constant pattern in David's Psalms. By this correlation, we comprehend that David is showing us not only the secret place but also the path to the secret place. Here we come to understand in our hearts what the refuge place in Christ is and what it means to be lifted up. Worship is the inner position that enables us to be lifted up; God is taking us to His refuge place. He is all along the One doing it through us; we must never forget that we do not know how to pray the rightful prayers (Rom. 8: 26-27). It is a secret place that no one can find; that is why we can call it a refuge place but no longer a secret place when you know it.

The mystery is revealed, and yet there are always new depths and heights that the Lord wants to show us and for us to explore in the refuge place. Therefore, they will remain a secret hiding place, always filled with new mysteries to fathom and explore. Through all of this, and because God is unchanging, we realize He is the ever-unchanging refuge. His shelter door is always open and ready to receive us. He is our shelter from the adversary, and in our shelter, under His wings, we are protected from accusation, slander, hurt, bitterness, lies, and all the things the world has to offer against us. We are being caught up when we are in that place; our spirit is being lifted up, and because of that, we are lifted deeper into His presence. Everything becomes obvious in and for us. Through this, we come to understand in a revelatory way in our hearts the different circumstances in life. We receive answered questions we carry in our hearts that only the Lord knows of. Spiritually what happens is that His light is being displayed in our lives (Num. 6:26). Because His light shines in our darkness, we come to understand that without His light shining upon us, we have no life because we carry no light or life.

Along with this understanding of our life, we are also being purged by His Spirit to handle more and more of His Light. A spiral of different aspects in God that has a constant effect on each other is when one moves, it touches another part, and that part will touch another. By this, the circle continuously moves deeper and deeper into His being because there are always more and deeper depths of God. In this place, spiritual issues become logical, and we understand that spiritual matters become physical matters (Gen. 1:3). We come to understand that these two, the spiritual and the physical, in everything are interconnected. Therefore, we grasp that everything in the Bible never contradicts itself but always connects. His Spirit reveals everything, layer by layer, just like the Bible when we read it; we read deeper and deeper into it.

> *Trust in, lean on, rely on, and have confidence in Him at all times, you people pour out your hearts before Him. God is a refuge for us (a fortress and a high tower). Selah [pause, and calmly think of that]! (Psalm 62:8)*

From a high tower, we can see what is going on; we can see something is going to happen out there. We can see things in the distance, and we can prepare ourselves for an attack and for incoming guests. The only place for us to be able to see what is taking place at any level in our life is through our inner watchman: the Holy Spirit. We have to understand the prevention of how to handle attacks so that we won't get killed spiritually, and we also have to learn to grasp when the unannounced guest is coming, the Holy Spirit. Often, He turns up unannounced, and a lot of times, we are not prepared. In growth, we need to be prepared all the time. We need to learn to recognize in our spirit when He is coming from a distance because we often fail to recognize Him and think it is an attack. We miss out on inviting in the Most Holy One. I'm trying to say that the Holy Spirit always displays Himself in a new way, especially when we are moving onto the next level. We can't clearly see who is coming at a distance, but we can see someone is coming. By this, we have to discern the difference between the Holy Spirit and the enemy at a distance. When Jesus walked on water, the disciples did not recognize Him at first and got scared. Even when the Lord spoke, they didn't recognize Him. Only after Peter requested the Lord to bid Him come did they recognize Him (Matt. 14:22-33). The Lord did something new, something they had never experienced from Him. In those moments, we must learn to discern. Another fact to remember is that a high tower was placed at the entrance next to the gates where they wrote all the laws. The law was made so that the people would know the difference between guest and enemy. What that means in the context of maturing in Christ is that if we don't know the law of God, then we will mistakenly invite the wrong thing into our lives.

Therefore, we must study the principles, statutes, and ordinances of God in the Bible because the carnal tends to address the physical matters first quickly and too long. Then, when we fail to find answers, we start to consider we need to go to God much later in the process.

> *Men of low degree [in the social scale] are emptiness (futility, a breath), and men of high degree [in the same scale] are a lie and a delusion. In the balances they go up; they are together lighter than a breath. (Psalm 62:9)*

What he is saying here is, don't trust men. They are like a vapor, like puff. Not rich, not poor. The poor have good intentions, but they can't fulfill them. And the rich promise a lot, but they can't fulfill it. They don't want to fulfill it. They lie - it's very interesting that he is writing that because they are mocking you. They pretend by saying, 'I want to help you', but when it comes down to it, rich people who have a lot are very self-sufficient. God uses people to help people. However, the longing to help people comes from the Spirit within. It does not lie in the indwelling part of the human heart from man itself. In other words, it is something God does through a person, which is why it says we should not trust men but God. God is using people, but we don't know who that is, so we should obey when the Lord tells us to do something.

David experienced very straining situations and many difficulties in his life. Still, through those situations, he found answers to life's circumstances. One of them he addresses here is not to trust the appearance of men. Another important point to take out in relation to our walk is that we must be cautious not to trust the carnal. It is not to be trusted because it leans on emotions of comfort. Another point in this matter is that the Lord wants us to trust Him first and foremost. He does send people along on our path to have companions. However, that is more the few than the many, just like it was with Jesus, He had three: Peter, James, and John (Mrk. 5:21-43 and Matt. 17:1-11).

> *Trust not in and rely confidently not on extortion and oppression, and do not vainly hope in robbery; if riches increase, set not your heart on them. (Psalm 62:10)*

Set not your heart on them - it means; don't put your heart in the rich(es), don't put your heart in wealth, or the ways to come about them because they won't last. The only riches that survive are those received from God: trust God. The ways David describes the riches gained are the downfalls we come by through them. Many would claim that they are not infatuated with riches. Still, if one examines the different motives through the carnal man, one very quickly finds how desperately weak the carnal man is for riches. This pattern applies in the same manner when it comes to prayer. When one experiences the wonderful manifestation of the Lord, visions, dreams, divine experiences, giftings, etc., the carnal man can easily fall into the trap of thinking that it is special and must be loved a little more than the rest of the herd. This is the fall of the riches in carnal nature. One must know that this is the nature of the carnal man and that it is a hindrance to be overcome through the dying in the arms of our beloved Lord.

> *God has spoken once, twice have I heard this: that power belongs to God. (Psalm 62:11)*

True strength is gained by being in close fellowship with the Lord. Not in the sense that we, in a carnal way, will gain power, but the mighty workings of the Lord through us; hence David is saying power belongs to God. Power is not determined by riches but by whether we seek His face, knowing that all power belongs to God. So one could reason by the mere thinking; a lump of clay can never gain any power.

> *Also to You, O Lord, belong mercy and loving-kindness, for You render to every man according to his work. (Psalm 62:12)*

Having the fear of God in the sense of being afraid of Him will make us hide things from Him, which will make us go into our own works unnoticed. The confidentiality with the Lord stops.

This has risen from carrying the fear of man out of wrong theology. We project the fear of man into our relationship with the Lord, and we act, think, and feel that this is what the fear of God looks like. If so, we must turn our hearts toward the depths of prayer and receive a revelation of His love for us. Out of this fact, we come to comprehend the right understanding of carrying the reverential fear of the Lord. It is birthed out of love. From this understanding, we find that He corrects us when we are on the wrong track of things. As the scripture says, He renders what we give out. He teaches us how to give and be in right standing before Him to receive justly. There seems to be a twisting in this matter of understanding what rightfully and righteous means. In terms of being rightful, seen from the carnal man's perspective of understanding God, it is when we think we do things rightfully, that we will receive what we have worked for. This will keep us having the fear of man because its origin has derived from the carnal man and therefore creates an unhealthy relationship with the Lord where we think we can buy our way into receiving His riches. Righteousness is to understand the seriousness in the precepts and order of the Lord, and in this, we come to have such deep love for Him. Here, its origin is of the Spirit. We receive the reverential fear of the Lord, then receive His inheritance for us.

The Lord is by all means and matter interested in all our affairs of life and that we are doing well. Therefore, He corrects us, sometimes harshly, because we are so off track, so we can come to live and experience the most glorious life here on earth and in heaven. As the scripture says, we come to understand that the Lord renders justly because He is the perfect expression of love. Therefore the correction He renders is perfect. Therefore, we can receive correction when we abide in the rightful understanding of the Lord's love for us. Even the difficult things are then receivable for us because His Spirit enables us to accept them and makes them spiritually logical. Thereby even in the nature of correction, we come to fathom the depths of taking refuge in Him; only He knows of just correction. All of which keeps us in His refuge.

# Chapter 8

# Taking on the Likeness of Jesus

**Sanctification: death of the carnal and resurrection of the spiritual authority**

When we grow, we grow into the likeness of Jesus – we grow in humbleness and synchronously with the fear of the Lord. These two are paired up. They are like a couple – you can't have one without the other. Out of this grows the understanding whereby we come to fathom the reason for our life: that we are growing into a vessel for prayer for His Spirit. We come to understand that He holds everything in His hands, timing in prayer for situations and things only He knows and holds. We become spiritually aware of this pattern in prayer.

Along with this, we also come to walk in the belief that He knows our every need, and because of this, we don't have to ask Him for needs because He knows. By this, we grasp His sovereignty for our small personal life. The fear of the Lord makes us realize everything has consequences, and when we ask, there is a price to pay. In His mercy and grace, if we pray out of the timing in His timing, nothing happens because He knows we are doing it out of ignorance. So first, from this point on, we start to become war prayers for Christ. It has been merely cleansing and purging all to gain spiritual authority until this point. Now we don't want our own life, but we have realized it is not life but a living stone that has been trying to live. At this point, we recognize spiritually that life only exists through Christ. The death of the carnal man starts, and life through Christ begins to shape us so that we can now be useful to Him. It is such a beautiful death of something that was never really alive. Out of this, the ease of letting go comes naturally; we no longer desire our will but only His.

> *[Come] and, like living stones, be yourselves built [into] a spiritual house, for a holy (dedicated, consecrated) priesthood, to offer up [those] spiritual sacrifices [that are] acceptable and pleasing to God through Jesus Christ. (1 Peter 2:5)*

Along with this purgation, we must undergo trials and testing before we are sent out and before we can be trusted with any power from God. He does not need to know, but it is for us to understand how we handle the responses and reactions under pressure. The only way to find out is under pressure. Therefore, we must go through the valley of the shadow of death.

We grow in maturity from these trials and testing because we will sit down and reflect on how we handled it. During this circle of growing in spiritual maturity, we realize that under pressure, we either grow straight toward Jesus or in the opposite direction.

When we grow in stature, He sends us out, so we understand that how we handle pressure is how we handle power. Both must have the same response, which is humbleness. This humbleness is laid as a foundation during the times of testing and trials. This realization is something we need to be dressed in before we are sent out.

All things are moved in the spiritual first. The first place to win a battle is in the spiritual realm. Therefore, we take on the burdens and carry our crosses before any happenings occur or before we will see any change in the physical. Carrying the burdens and bearing our crosses is where the spiritual work is being done. Here we come to fathom that we are not fighting against flesh and blood but against spiritual powers (Eph. 6:12). What is working against us is not people in the physical realm or situations that suddenly come against us. No, here we realize the reality of the principalities and powers working against us.

Here starts the spiritual fight against it, which is called intercessory prayer, which is our mighty weapon. We learn how to put on the whole armor of God (Eph. 6:11). This is needed. Otherwise, we will not learn to defeat the principalities working against us. Here we learn to understand that it is not people coming against us but that it is the enemy. Therefore, here we learn to pray for our enemies. We learn to wait on and trust God.

He will turn the difficult situations around because we have realized He is the only authority higher and greater than the workings of the spiritual principalities coming against us. We understand that the powers coming against us are beyond our reach because we fathom what kind of power is working against us. They truly are powers that we can never battle with; they surpass every attempt we could ever make. This is how Jesus fought and won every battle He faced. He understood the workings of the spiritual realm. This we must do likewise; come fully to terms with that we can only survive in the arms of Christ.

*Elena Radef*

# HOW TO GROW IN THE LIKENESS OF JESUS

## Chapter 9

# Walking in God's Power

**Being led by His presence, the subtle inner change**

There are layers of growing Christ-like, and we must not become discouraged when we reach this next point, which I will describe. It is a place where we need to be steadfast without being able to see any change for quite some time. It is a place of training our faith in our personal prayer life, like a desert landscape without any ends where we continuously search for water. We have come a little further down the Christian walk when we reach this point because there has to be a certain depth of loving Jesus more than life to endure the desert. During these times, we come to fathom how much we can endure. It is very pleasing to Him when we endure suffering and trials to receive the reward of glory. At some point, there'll arise the frustration on the inside, which would be described as coming to the ends of ourselves. It appears from the knowledge that we want to experience and live in the glory of God in every part of our lives. Still, the flesh seems to invent a formula for how this wandering will be, but it has derived this from the world and is therefore useless.

Previously before reaching this point, we have had glimpses of closeness with the Lord. We deeply long for a lasting lifestyle in communion with the Lord. We are deeply longing and searching for whatever change is needed for this to happen, which is often referred to as a breakthrough. Out of this deep sadness, desperation and frustration arise. The longing is within our nature to seek God, which He has laid within us, but the workings out of them are not something the carnal man can touch to change. In the trying to follow the rules, the carnal realizes at some point, when exhausted enough, that it's working is not compliable. A lot of time may pass before discovering that the world's ways do not apply. The Lord shows us by His grace that it is not something we can work our way into other than that we must die. To keep walking in the desert is the only place we can receive the trust we need to walk in faith.

The destress on the inside regarding this is that we are in a constant battle, trying to tame the feelings that are arising, longing to walk in the glory of God, but it never seems to happen. So, we try to stay content (notice trying is not the same as being content). We say to ourselves that perhaps it was not meant for me to live in the river of God's abundance in life. We don't want to say it out loud because we don't want to sound like an ungrateful and failing Christian. However, this inner agony becomes stronger. We use a tremendous amount of time and energy to battle this mental tendency on the inside. We have no idea how much time and energy we use on it because we have lived in this fashion our whole lives because of the carnal man's character of never really believing anything good is lasting, which is true in the world and through the carnal.

This is how the Lord teaches us that His abundance is lasting, removing doubt and replacing it with His faith—realizing that only through Christ Jesus can we live a life of lasting goodness. But unfortunately, this often takes years for us to grasp and comprehend, equally long for the carnal man to die.

I am writing abundance as a means to express God's ways of showing His love for us. The way He does it is by giving and fulfilling our needs making them overflow in our lives so that we can reach out to others.

Abundance in Hebrew means greatness, more, multiplied, plentiful, numerous, large amount, extent, increased, mighty, great number, great quantity, etc. We receive this in all areas of our life - not in one area.

When walking in a desert landscape, we must understand that we are taking one step at a time and that each step consists of increased faith. It never decreases when we keep walking. When we have walked for a while, we can look back on our trail; by that, we can see we have walked at a certain piece. This is the only reference point we have. We can't feel faith. We have to do the action required to increase in faith. When we walk, our muscles become stronger and stronger, all-in order to endure more walking, and suddenly we don't mind walking a little longer. This is the point where our focus can rest on the Lord. By this, we come to fathom that this is the Christian walk with our Lord. We grasp how we are dying to the carnal nature to the point of no return. We know this because we forget ourselves and get occupied with the face of the Lord. We stop thirsting for physical water but crave spiritual water. We walk and get to know more about the ways of the Lord and the deeper presence of Him we can grow into. I should say it increases into a place where we know how to open the door to enter into the constant presence of Christ, and yet at the same time never take it for granted. I find it to be a mystery. The working of the Holy Spirit within is a delicate matter.

The Bible says we won't faint or grow weary when we are constantly seeking His presence to overcome the dry areas of our Christian walk (Isa. 40:31). God will respond because that's His nature. We are His children, and He is our Father. Therefore, God will respond to all of His children.

When we realize that it is not something we can produce, we start to enter the rest of peace in prayer. Then waiting on Him becomes all we want, and it is no longer something we feel we have to wait for. On the contrary, we wait on Him - through waiting is communion. As one can see, we have to come to terms with understanding that the ways of the Lord are very different from the way we operate in the system of the world. This takes time because the Holy Spirit needs to work it through us:

- Renewing our mind
- Taking us through purgation
- Shaping us
- Tearing down the old carnal man
- Building us up

- Living it through our inner man

The purified soul has always been there, understanding that the reformation of man is what is needed and then positioning everything within it in the correct order. Walking in His glory requires the death of the carnal man, as opposed to the way the carnality steered us before our conversion. This includes our emotional and physical attachment to the body, imaginations, phantasies, and our mind: fear, joy, sadness, longing, desire, lust, anger, serenity, etc., of the flesh. All these traits need to be renewed and redirected toward Christ. Transformed into the life Christ has set out for us; the inner purgation and transformation into the image of Christ, a handed over life to Christ, to renew every area of our life. As one can see, this does not happen overnight, but it is a purgation process we undergo.

Along with this, there will be times and places in our life where there is dry land; the dry land resembles a place where the transformation of the flesh needs to take place for an increase of faith. If we want a plant to grow, we have to water it; if we want a plant to die, we must stop watering it. This pattern we recognize in our Christin walk, and only Christ knows when we have died in all these areas. The depths of each area are only revealed to Christ because He knows the innermost being of our heart, and we don't.

Remember when Peter said to the Lord; I will never leave you, and within the morning, he had denied Him three times just like the Lord had prophesied to Him. Peter was quite sure of himself, which is the carnal's nature (Matt. 26:35).

Again, we see one of the main traits of the Lord that He is always showing us; we can't make it without Him. We cannot undergo this purgation ourselves. This is not a psychological treatment in depth; this is the beginning of the resurrection of Christ within.

# Chapter 10

# Impatience, Worry, and Fear make us Withdraw

**Waiting in His presence purges the carnal from emotional defaults**

Impatience is an emotion that the carnal man is steering. If not dealt with, it can lead to a downfall in various degrees, even to the point of falling away from the Lord. One could say it is a default in the carnal man's nature that needs the correction of God to be turned into patience, which we can see only through the purgation of the Holy Spirit.

First, we need to understand the great force working along with our weak carnal man, which is Satan. We can now see how it is impossible for us to turn impatience into patience.

Secondly, we must understand that impatience abides naturally in the carnal man. We must overcome these two barriers, which we can see are impossible for us to change. Realizing this matter is the first step toward turning impatience into patience. Finally, we must understand that the ability to have patience is a trait that can only grow forth in a healthy and lasting condition through the Holy Spirit. Hence He is the only one who carries the fulfillment of patience because He is patient. The fruits of the Holy Spirit clearly state that fact (Gal. 5:22-23). Therefore, we must, by all means, seek the source of the character we are looking for; the Holy Spirit. This implies that we cannot turn to our understanding of grasping the matter through ourselves or the world because it doesn't abide there. And if it only lies within the fruits of the Holy Spirit, we do not carry that trait. Now that we have stated the origin of patience, we can begin to take the affairs in the rightful order.

We all desire to be able to fill the mark of patience. The desire to seek patience is laid within us. We must realize that we do not own the ability to turn impatience into patience because that quality is a love so vast and deep that we see we do not have that lasting trait. We only experience smaller degrees of patience, drops of it, but not lasting and turned around within. We have tasted all the fruits of the Holy Spirit, but we have not come to produce the fruits, so we seek and long in the Holy Spirit for this to happen, which is the whole purpose.

Addressing the matter of impatience regarding prayer life, it is of utmost importance that we understand that to receive patience. The Lord trains us through situations and in our prayer time to build patience within. Training has to do with building our spiritual character and muscles - understanding that in our carnal nature, we see that it fathoms itself to be strong and built like a mature spiritual person when it has no real vision or comprehension of the truth. It is living and abiding under such great deceit, unaware that it is not right and firmly secure. When we understand that this is how disillusioned the carnal man sees itself and lives by, strong in its own belief and unable to recognize the deceit, we have the right starting point to take off from. This pattern of falling back into old tendencies of the carnal man is right at hand, especially concerning prayer life. There is a great distinction between how we perceive handling our prayer life and our walk with the Lord - as if we can treat them differently, which we cannot. Our prayer life is the source of keeping us on the right track. In life, we understand that we need to run our race, and that's done by moving forward with the Lord, but when it comes to prayer life, tendencies are much more likely to try to do things by ourselves. We think we run our race well when in fact, we are moving backward without our knowledge. Often, falling away from walking with the Lord in prayer arises from not waiting on Him but asking Him to hurry to come. We need to run our race forward with patience, not by going backward, through the impatience of the carnal (Heb.12 1-3).

Impatience in prayer life shows up in a manner of losing sight very quickly of the promises from God. Somehow the weakness in the carnal man is that it equals a quick solution or outcome for it to be right. The frame box of putting the Lord on a time schedule is right at hand, forgetting we cannot tell the maker to shape the situation (Isa. 45:11, Rom. 9:20). Impatience with time is a powerful tendency and weakness in the carnal man. Therefore, when it takes time, sometimes even for God to appear in prayer life, it moves into thinking something is wrong and gets impatient. This shows that when prayer comes, even from the slightest tendency of a carnal man, it will lead to impatience regarding time. Impatience is often brought forth by fear. The flesh lacks the knowledge of being fine with not knowing when. Only through the Holy Spirit can we handle not knowing when - out of the peace in the Holy Spirit. The way for the flesh to handle situations is to get it over and done with: impatience. The flesh is always in a hurry, it is the nature of the carnal man, and this is what needs workings in the mighty hands of our Lord.

We must contemplate that getting a good solid great oak tree requires a lot of time to unfold in its right and grandeur settings. We know that an oak tree cannot grow in haste, but it grows over time, moving through different seasons to make it strong and enduring. This is how we should contemplate our spiritual growth. It takes much longer than we realize. And in this matter, understand that we most of all learn to trust, to walk faithfully in His love for us. This is the foundation of patience. From impatience arises prefixed thinking that the carnal is using in order not to wait in patience in situations in life, but also regarding God's promises, especially those directed toward our personal life. The flesh is weak and foolish because it thinks it has insight. By this knowledge, the flesh is truly an enmity to God. Through impatience, we no longer pray in confidence in the Lord; by turning our eyes on Him confidently, knowing the faithfulness of His nature. Instead, we have turned our eyes upon the carnal nature for help.

> *For those who are according to the flesh and are controlled by its unholy desires set their minds on and pursue those things which gratify the flesh, but those who are according to the Spirit and are controlled by the Spirit set their minds on and seek those things which gratify the [Holy] Spirit. Now the mind of the flesh [which is sense and reason without the Holy Spirit] is death [death that comprises all the miseries arising from sin, both here and*

*hereafter]. But the mind of the [Holy] Spirit is life and [soul] peace [both now and forever] [That is] because the mind of the flesh [with its carnal thoughts and purposes] is hostile to God, for it does not submit itself to God's law; indeed it cannot. So then those who are living the life of the flesh [catering to the appetites and impulses of their carnal nature] cannot please or satisfy God, or be acceptable to Him. (Romans 8:5-8)*

Understanding that impatience is the foundation of the carnal man needs to be very clear; that we in no way can trust the nature of the carnal man. We must recognize and repent from this matter, and then we must understand that we cannot grasp the workings of the Lord because we are carnal. This is one of the foundational building blocks that need to be laid within our inner beings. For a camel to go through a needle's eye requires that it becomes really small. That's what we need to become in prayer, really small, and then we can come through the eye of a needle. The way to become small is by recognizing that we can only do it with God (Matt. 19:24). When something is small, it moves slowly. That is why we wait on and yield to the Lord in prayer. There is timing in prayer, in which we can never be in a hurry. When something is small, it requires our attention to navigate. We cannot hasten a small child, and it needs that we have the time to wait. It is the same in yielding. The flesh is like a small child, really slow to walk and comprehend everything that is going on around it. A small child moves slowly while learning to walk. Spiritually our growth is the same when we meet Christ. We must be like a small child to become more mature in Christ.

We are never adults in Christ but children, learning our whole life.

## Worry and fear

A second great hindrance worth mentioning is worry and fear during prayer time. It can be of such a great hindrance and such a disturbance to come into the position of yielding. The nature of the carnal man works is that it thinks it needs to get the issues of life in order before it can relax, and when this is in place, it thinks it can move into yielding. It thinks the issues of life need to be in order or to have an orderly life before entering a place of yielding. This mainly implies worry and fear before moving into the depth of prayer. Living an orderly and decent life through the nature of the carnal man equals no worry and fear, which is true but only done through the workings of the Holy Spirit in our sanctification process. In the failings of the carnal man, it thinks that it is something it can perform - what a terrible mistake.

One has to realize that it is, in fact, quite contrary to the workings of the Lord and the Holy Spirit. Nevertheless, this trait is part of the old life, and the old nature is needed to be recognized as part of the old man.

The depth of worry and fear varies a lot in prayer, but no matter its depth, it is such a great hindrance and disturbance that we need to be quite strict about handling it. It should have absolutely no foothold on the inner by giving into it. The variation can range from worrying about not forgetting things for later during the day, to becoming so anxious about settings and situations in our life, that the fear completely overtakes us. So much so, we no longer can stay in prayer and start moving around in fear, deeply disturbed. In all these affairs, which vary in-depth, we must remember even in the slightest thoughts of worry, anxiety, and fear, the devil, works his mighty works, cheering on with his minions for us to stay in this state. We need to combat this immediately when it arises, even in the slightest bit. By remembering the devil is cheering us to fall and cheering on the weakness of the carnal man, we can see the importance of a renewed mind. It is the only thing that enables us to combat the thoughts the devil suggests to us during prayer time. During prayer time, it is easy to fathom the workings of our mind. The intensity of worry and fear can be so overwhelming that they seem to be the only reality left. And the recipe is to move into worship. When we sing, the atmosphere changes. We see this spiritual work done when David was called to minister to Saul whenever an evil spirit would enter Saul (1 Sam. 16:14-23).

The Lord has given us a mouth, among others, for this reason. We were created to sing to the Lord. When we sing from our hearts to the Lord, we let out prayers in a different way. There is always a response from the Lord when we pray from our hearts. Paul addresses this affair (Eph. 5:19). There are spiritual occurrences taking place when we worship. Right before Jesus and the disciples left after the last supper, they sang hymns (Matt. 26:30). We must understand that worship and singing are spiritual weapons, and the devil cannot influence us when we worship. He cannot induce us with his deceptive thoughts and therefore hates worship. Right before Jesus went on the most important mission laid out before Him, He spent His time with the disciples singing hymns. That tells us of the utmost important influence that praise and worship have. Jesus is teaching us a principle; right before we go on our mission, whatever that may be, we need to praise and worship the Lord. Jesus always thanked the Father for hearing His prayers before He did anything, thanking Him for taking care of the situation. This He could do because He only did what the Father told Him to do. Therefore, there is only thanksgiving left. This is how the Lord has called us to walk with Him. We clearly know how contrary the carnal would react to a situation like this. The carnal man's reaction to being sentenced to death would not be singing but remorse. The only people that react with worship when they are about to die are the people of God, Holy Spirit-filled people. We see this displayed with the death of Stephen. He worshipped the Lord and prayed for those stoning him. He saw heaven open and the Son of Man standing at the right hand of God. He was abiding in the reality of the Lord (Acts 7:54-56).

There is no room for thinking when singing with a heart full of desire and desperation for the Lord. It is impossible to sing and think at the same time, which is the whole point and the reason for us to sing because when we are deeply immersed in our singing, the devil cannot influence us with worry and fear. When the Lord responds to our singing, He comes and enthrones us (Psa. 22:3). One could say He is entering the scene. That also means we receive a response from the Lord: a word, peace, an unction, or something else. He will for sure respond at some point. We need to learn to wait and keep praising Him until we receive a response from Him.

One time I was in such a crisis. I felt terrible. My life was a wreck, and all I could hear was the devil's voice cheering me on in my mind. The only thing the Lord kept saying to me was, "worship me right now." Now, I did not feel like worshipping Him, I was fearful, angry, hurt, and bitter, but I did it because I was desperate for Him. What happened was that within 15 minutes, I was full of the joy of the Lord. My life situation did not change right away, but I learned the mighty weapon of worshipping Him. Over time the Lord restored the situation. The Lord often places us in situations to learn to use the weapon of worship to move into peace. We learn that worrying is the opposite of faith, and the Lord is training us to walk in faith by taking us out of fear and worry. Worrying belongs to the carnal man; Jesus explicitly tells us not to worry (Matt. 6:25-34). This we can do because we walk with the Almighty Lord. I understand why people worry when they don't walk with the Lord, I would say there is a reason to worry then. It takes time to learn not to worry and to trust in the Lord because the carnal is so used to worrying about all kinds of issues in life. When we walk with the Lord, we learn and see how He deals with the occurrences in life that we are worrying about. It is a partnership we are entering into, not on equal terms. On the contrary, we must rely on the fact that He knows what it takes and is telling us what to do and when to do it. This is the principle we see when Jesus tells us not to worry:

> *But seek (aim at and strive after) first of all His kingdom and His righteousness, (His way of doing and being right), and then all these things taken together will be given you besides. (Matthew 6:33)*

There are some things in my life the Lord changed right away, and there are some things I am still waiting for Him to move on. However, I have learned that He knows the timing in all affairs because I have seen Him change situations in my life when the need arose.

Much of this applies likewise regarding fear. 365 times the Bible tells us not to fear. One for each day. We need to hear it every day because there is always something igniting fear in us. It takes a lot of tarrying with the Lord and a lot of training to learn to abide in His peace. When we do the things the Lord asks of us, we know it is no longer in our hands, and the fear of the situation ceases because we fathom it is out of our hands. This is a major key to overcoming fear. We should, however, always be on guard in examining ourselves. We learn that when the comfort of the carnal takes over, we should quickly turn to Lord on the inner; we learn never to trust ourselves. If we walk in the footsteps of Christ, this will occur as a natural consequence. Worry and fear often of times go hand in hand. So, if you take hold of the one, you will take hold of the other.

# Chapter 11

# Understanding the Righteousness of God

**Being in right standing with God**

The righteousness of Christ placed us in right standing before God, bought with the highest price from our blessed Lord. When we understand this, we reach a point where we no longer want to hide any parts of our life from Christ. On the contrary, we would most long for us to show all of us because we realize that we can fully and solemnly trust Him. A major inner spiritual shift takes place, and by this, we come to abide deeper within Him. When the knowledge of the righteousness given by Christ in our hearts merges as truth, we can then stand before Him and surrender all of our lives to Him. We have reached a point where we know that right standing before God has only to do with what Jesus did on the Cross and nothing to do with us. The knowledge of trust arises, and therefore it becomes easy to show everything of ourselves to Him because, in this realization, we come to grasp His love for us. Of course, we will never completely understand God's love for us. But here, we reach the point of understanding His love for us in a way where we cross a line of not holding anything back from Him. This enables us, with a longing, to show everything of ourselves to Him.

We have finally come to comprehend that His leadership and correction are done through love. This ends all performance that lies within the carnal nature. Here we fathom in a revelatory way that He is omniscient, the Leader, the Provider of everything, and His righteousness upholds all life (1 Tim. 6:13). This knowledge makes our trust grow into a place where we can solemnly put our heads on His bosom, close our eyes, and trust Him. It takes time to fathom that He will never leave us, years of growing in trust, and hence years of dying to the carnal nature. Being in right standing with God enables us to show and give everything of ourselves to Him. Without the revelation, we are unable, from lack of trust, because the carnal man does not carry this trait of surrendering our life to Him.

We also fathom we cannot produce this trust that enables us to surrender; again, we grasp that it is the workings of the Holy Spirit. Here we understand that we can only come to stand before the Lord when we are in right standing with God, meaning it is He enabling us to be in right standing. We can only handle standing before Him when He positions us. The carnal man is what takes time to die to because it is not in its nature to surrender and trust completely. The carnal man is like a donkey, very timid and stubborn in its own ways. The timidness is tied to the difficulty of surrendering completely; it takes a lot of time to learn to trust the Lord. The stubbornness is tied to its thinking that it knows better than its master. The workings of the world and the adversary are working in the same direction. Nothing except our dear Lord wants this freedom for us and, thereby, the only One who is its provider. Doings and workings do not produce righteousness or being in right standing with God. The righteousness of Christ is given freely and cannot be earned, hence the free provision given by Jesus Christ in which He fulfilled the Old Testament law on the Cross. We must consider this matter carefully; we must pay close attention to this default in the carnal man. It somehow perceives itself as being in right standing with God on its own terms, mostly from the reading of the Word and interpreting it through a carnal mind.

The results in prayer have a likewise pattern if not dealt with; the carnal mind interprets, and by this, the carnal mind prays. The carnal man often needs to surrender to the matter in contemplation that Jesus, given freely through grace, provided the righteousness. These affairs take a lifetime to sink deep within, and they are without end. We must consider the affair of the adversary in these matters: he is very sneaky, subtle, and brings forth very good arguments of why things and matters seem to be from the Lord. So likewise does the flesh; we must pay attention to the agenda in the things we do because the flesh likes to put itself upfront out of pride.

## Chapter 11: Understanding the Righteousness of God

*For it is by free grace (God's unmerited favor) that you are saved (delivered from judgment and made partakers of Christ's salvation) through [your] faith. And this [salvation] is not of yourselves [of your own doing, it came not through your own striving], but it is the gift of God; Not because of work's [not the fulfillment of the Law's demands], lest any man should boast. [It is not the result of what anyone can possibly do, so no one can pride himself in it or take glory to himself]. (Ephesians 2:8-9)*

A prayer coming from works is the working of the carnal man that thinks it can earn its way. This takes place on the inner in a very subtle way. The reason for these affairs is the carnal has derived from the perception that behaving well must eventually produce a deeper intimate relationship with the Lord. It somehow equals the action with the result. All of these are works of the Old Testament. Another trademark in regards to this is how the carnal man is boasting itself sometimes in small remarks or ways of behaving, exclaiming how good a behavior it has, as a way of making itself participate in the workings of the Lord. Notice, it does it in a subtle way for it to look humble - we must pay close attention (Matt. 6:5). The carnal man compares the good to the good of the world and only has a certain amount of capability of knowing what good means. It has no clue what good means in God's eyes, but it is foolishly confident that it does. A weakness of the carnal man is that it can only compare to what it already knows; the ways and workings of the world. Yet it compares what it knows to the ways and workings of the Lord. Even the terminology of acting good is of the world. When we act before God, it should be turned in the direction of rightful.

We must know that the only way to be able to act rightfully is first through the revelation of our righteousness from Christ because of what He did on the Cross. Secondly, by the Holy Spirit within this comes supernaturally; what was difficult becomes easy because of Christ. It is not something we can produce; what a misconception to even come close to thinking that we can act rightfully when we are merely but a living stone, a vessel God has brought to life. What can a vessel produce? Nothing, but only by the grace of God do we come to live. Being righteous before God is solemnly given by the grace of God.

Regarding others in this matter, we must consider that we are all at different levels in our walk with Christ. Therefore, we cannot look at where people are and judge what they are doing when they are doing it and how they are doing it. We must be cautious in bringing forth opinions about their situation and living. Because of all the misconceptions in this area, there is a lot that needs to be restored in the body of Christ. We must heed the opinionated affairs of the carnal man because it thinks it knows and understands much when in fact, it comprehends so very little (Matt. 26:41). This we can especially see in the affairs of how it treats other members of the body of Christ. It seems to forget that what we do to others, we do to Him. (Matt. 25:31-40). By this judgmental behavior of the carnal man, there has risen a lack of love in the church for the brotherhood, for those who don't act in a certain Christian way, which is often defined by dos and don'ts from the world. The enemy still has a foothold in the church in this area. The comparison toward each other is one of the ways the enemy holds the Christians prisoners. Of course, he knows this and uses it very well in a subtle and sneaky way. He performs these subtle affairs, keeps the Christians prisoners, and makes them unable to receive their blessings from the Lord. The spiritual law that is at stake here is when holding back in receiving others out of judgment; we hold back on receiving what the Lord has in store for us because we are doing it toward Him and not the other person. It always sounds justified in the mind of the carnal man when we have an opinion toward others, which is why we must know the Word of God. What can one vessel know about another vessel apart from being a vessel in itself? Can one vessel guide and be a leader to something similar? I know the Bible talks about for us to rebuke a brother when he is about to fall, but that is a whole other matter. Many miss and conceptualize these two. People are eager to tell people what to do when nobody asks them. We need to talk with them and listen instead of bringing forth opinions. Suspiciousness often arises before trust, gossip, and slander, which must be restored in the church.

# Chapter 12

# Knowing God is Omnipresent

**He was and is ever-present in our lives**

God is always there in His omnipotent presence. When we live from this point of view in life, with this knowledge in our hearts, we know we are never alone, and under any circumstance, we can always talk and confide in God. We live in the revelation of His magnitude, power, and greatness. We understand that it is one trait that nobody else in the world can fulfill.

In the matter of old hurts, this makes the difference because God is the only one who is our all and can mend all brokenness, hence Him being omnipotent, omnipresent, and omniscient. Through all the trials and tribulations, He was always with us. Not one incident He missed out on in our whole life. He has been in every circumstance of our life. Even when we think nobody was there, Jesus was there and therefore is the only one that can guide us through every situation. He knows every word that needs to be spoken, what inner healing and every action are needed for us to set us free. One main theme that moves along in these old past hurts is loneliness. In most of them, we were left in a position of loneliness. It is important to contemplate that it boils down to that.

Receiving a revelation of His omnipresence breaks down the massive stronghold that most people struggle with, loneliness. Most people struggle with this of some sort. All derived from past hurts. The devil always wants us to think that we are the only one who feels lonely. So he uses it against us. I'm moving more depth in this matter in the chapter "Psychological influence from the past."

The realization that the Lord was always there moves us to a very important position, where we can repent and forgive. Repent from believing these stories about us and acting them out, forgive those who hurt us, and make us believe we are lonely and that something is wrong with us. These two go together.

Unforgiveness is like a veil in front of our eyes, and there are two angels to this:

1. The unforgiveness toward the other person keeps us in bondage. Sometimes we don't even remember the story of what happened correctly, but often, the story gets even worse over time when told numerous times, which usually will create more anger. Anger and hurt create bitterness in our hearts. This will eventually spread to the rest of our life so that we won't experience any joy in any area, and we feel that the whole world is against us.

2. The unforgiveness toward ourselves places us in a position where we stay angry at ourselves. Out of this grows more shame, guilt, and loneliness. A lot of self-justification and self-righteousness grow from being in this hurt of unforgiveness. We must understand that the carnal man's only tool is self-justification and self-righteousness. Forgiveness is only something that the Holy Spirit can do through us. Therefore, the carnal man falls short of itself.

The Bible clearly states that we should forgive our enemies because it sets us free (Matt. 5:43, 6:12). It is easy to forgive the ones we love, but forgiving our enemies is another matter. That is what Jesus did with us. He restored the relationship to the Father, us being His worst enemies, and set us free. The same is displayed in a miniature version when we forgive, understanding that forgiveness can occur only through the Holy Spirit.

The knowledge of never being alone at any moment in our lives enables us to lean on Christ. Because in confiding in Him, we receive the help needed for all difficult situations we ever were in. This provides an emotional, mental, and spiritual comfort that enables us to keep going through the layers of old hurt to be restored. Loneliness is one of the primary attacks the enemy wants to place as a stronghold in our lives as early as possible. By this, we lose the ability to trust. By this, it can be very straining and difficult for us to come to the Lord.

## Chapter 12: Knowing God is Omnipresent

*But the Comforter (Counselor, Helper, Intercessor, Advocate, Strengthener, Standby), the Holy Spirit, Whom the Father will send in My name [in My place, to represent me and act on My behalf], He will teach you all things. And he will cause you to recall (will remind you of, bring to your remembrance) everything I have told you. (John 14:26)*

'But God,' the Bible often writes, meaning He supersedes all things, matters, and affairs. He becomes our all because He is all: I Am yesterday, today, and forever. I Am the Alpha and the Omega beginning and the end of all things. He is the restorer of our hearts, the remover of infliction in the heart. Only He can perform such a delicate task; He is our Healer. When we know that God is omnipresent and that He is ever-present with us, an inner rest and peace come to our lives. When He is letting us know by His presence that He will never leave us, there arises such a life of security in Him, to such a degree that we can taste the life of glory He has provided for us. The darkness of the carnal man, the darkness of the old life, ceases, and we experience the life of light within, the new creation, the Holy Spirit. The knowledge of the Lord's omnipresence in all of our lives directly influences our purgation and prayer life. It enables us to open up to Him regarding all of the old hurts so that they can be purged because the knowledge of Him being present makes Him the remedy. A natural surrender can take place.

# Chapter 13

# The Impact of the Psychological Influence from the Past

**Affects our relationship with the Lord**

In terms of our previous life, before conversion, we have been exposed to hurtful relationships that sometimes cause excruciating pain in our hearts. In addition, those hurtful family and friend experiences leave us unable to comprehend life in healthy relationships.

We may not understand that we can only have good healthy relationships when the three-cord string is present: The Lord, us, and the third party. We might be able to picture them differently in our minds. Still, the wrongful coding in our hearts makes it impossible to change to where we are free from the past hurtful event, enabling us to live in a healthy relationship. Some people have been hurt in friendships but have no particular problems with having a loving spouse. But each of us has had a relationship situation that seemed unchangeable no matter how hard we tried to rectify it.

If we are unaware of the painful hurts in our hearts, those scars will hinder our relationship with the Lord. It could take many years to work through those past hurts. We must confront our past hurts to deepen our relationship with Him. Many of us have had parents that were more attentive to themselves than parenting us, which leaves us in a state of insecurity and makes us unable to trust. When we enter a relationship with the Lord, this emotional insecurity will rise to the top.

We will project onto our relationship with the Lord old emotional hurt on Him and thereby in the relationship. We cannot see His love for us clearly in a sense that we don't, at the bottom of our hearts, dare even to lean into trusting Him because we project out all our old hurts. We must come to terms with love equals trust. Pointing this affair out very specifically is very important because many people struggle to hand their hearts over to Christ. We must understand that in a loving relationship, everything is laid at the altar; nothing is hidden away in fear that the other will find out about this problem we have and might leave us. The greatest deceit of the carnal man we carry is that it thinks that when it is not confronting itself in being honestly truthful, the problem might go away. The carnal man abides in a fantasy world regarding matters of old hurt. It thinks that someone or somebody will come and save them and that they don't have to do anything. In this affair, the carnal man has never been trained to do any mindful uplifting to move out of the old hurt; it is slothful out of fear.

One could argue that it holds truth to the sense of someone saving them, which is right; we need a Savior but fail to understand, out of lack of knowledge and training, the workings of their part. The carnal mind must steer into understanding the importance of taking action and move out of the slothfulness of fear. The only way we can change this heart position back into trust is through Jesus. This is why we should not try to do this by ourselves. The only one who will not fail in this is Jesus. He went through all pain and agony (Matt. 8:17), so we don't have to live in it. Not to say we won't experience pain and suffering, but He is our way out of them: emotionally, mentally, and spiritually. No one else can touch people's lives on all three accounts. He is our great physician, healer, and restorer. To some small degree, we might think to know intellectually what is good, healthy, and sound, when in reality, we can only see through Him because He is the full expression of life, and we cannot fight the demons hunting us from our past. We know they are there and that they are not good for us. But it seems that no matter how hard we try, we can't change. Perhaps we even tried many things to change them but never succeeded, seemingly like the women with the issue of blood (Luk. 8:43-48). The Bible tells us that she had used all her money and sought every physician, but nothing helped. This affair we can easily recognize. Since the Spirit of God is the Highest power to move and alter all matters and affairs, He naturally becomes the only source of salvation and is the One we must turn to.

*Chapter 13: The Impact of the Psychological Influence from the Past*

It is for us to understand by heart in a revelatory way the power there is in the name of Jesus. It is not like any other name; it is the name above all other names, meaning it is the highest authority in the universe (Phil. 2:9, Eph. 1:21, Matt. 28:18).

Therefore, He is the only one who can set us free because He is the only one who can enter our hearts and heal them because He truly loves us, which He displayed by the great passion on the Cross.

There is, therefore, no problem that is too big for God. We might think there is because the problem seems so immense that we can't see its end. Especially problems from childhood may seem so excruciatingly painful, and we might even understand to some degree that we are far-fetched in our minds. So, we think, how will I ever come to any clarity and solve the problem? Jesus cured the man filled with a legion of demons. Nobody else could restrain him or help him. A legion rage from 3000-6000. That tells us this man had a massive problem before he could be restored. (Mrk. 5:1-29). The analogy in this story is the gigantic unfathomable problem being restored in a way we don't understand. He was even cured instantaneously when the right timing was there. The man became so fond of Jesus that he wanted to go with Him. In the realization of Jesus being His redeemer, he gave his life to Him by saying, "can I come with you?"

He came to know Jesus is the highest authority and came to know Him because he saw His love displayed for Him. He probably never thought for a second that he deserved to be saved. Most likely, being demon-possessed, he had hurt many people and thought he could never be saved. And afterward, Jesus told him to go and preach the Gospel, telling them about what He had done. He also sent him home to people who knew him and restored everything that was lost to him. We see the importance of becoming keenly aware of patterns from our life before our conversion. If not dealt with, they will be a hindrance to us.

# THE REALITY OF INTIMATE PRAYER LIFE

## Chapter 14

# Understanding the Intimate Prayer Life

**Purgation assists and lead us to stay spiritually awake**

A significant realization we must come to is that without the Holy Spirit, we cannot pray properly, (Rom 8:23-27) makes this very clear. There is no misunderstanding about that. It is one of our weaknesses, and we must understand this first, and then we can enter into a deep intimate prayer life. What a misunderstanding to think that we should be able to pray when it is, in fact, a quality we don't own; therefore, we are unable. It is the Holy Spirit that prays through us. Through scripture, we come to understand the workings of the Holy Spirit and that He is longing to use us in prayer, unfolding what it means to have a deep-rooted intimate prayer life.

> *And not only the creation, but we ourselves too, who have and enjoy the firstfruits of the [Holy] Spirit [a foretaste of the blissful things to come] groan inwardly as we wait for the redemption of our bodies [from sensuality and the grave, which will reveal] our adoption (our manifestation as God's sons). (Romans 8:23)*

By the Holy Spirit, we get the first fruits of what Christ redeemed for us to enjoy, walk in, and have. A foretaste of what is to come, and this is what we get to experience in prayer; a foretaste of heaven. The Holy Spirit groans inwardly through us, and in that, the Holy Spirit groans for us to have a deep intimate relationship with Him. Groaning is beyond words and expression; it is the Holy Spirit's longing that we should develop a personal relationship with Him. Therefore, when we allow the Holy Spirit to take over in prayer, we grow into the likeness of Jesus; our whole inner being, soul, and mind come into the shape and form of Christ. We are being molded into His image, which is the entire point. And when we consciously and spiritually understand that it is the Holy Spirit taking over in prayer, there comes a shift of perception in our inner man. We come to know that it is never us making the prayers function, but it is always the product of the Holy Spirit.

Here is a picture of how prayer works and who we are regarding the Holy Spirit in prayer. We are like a dirty piece of glass placed under the sun. Therefore, when we pray and the Holy Spirit starts to pour itself on us, depicted as light coming through the window, very little light can come through it at first. For us to become a clean piece of glass, we have to spend time in prayer. This is the washing of the glass. In the end, we can become a clean piece of glass through which the Holy Spirit can shine His light. So, understanding that we can only become so transparent as glass, therefore, we must conclude that it is always the mighty workings of the Holy Spirit: in prayer, in life, in purgation, in sanctification, and so forth.

This can also make up for the affairs if things are being hindered. Then we must conclude that we hinder and never the Spirit. If so happens, we must seek deeper, wait and yield in His presence for an inner shift that takes place spiritually. We must also remember that the Lord moves through life on a different schedule than that carnal man. Here patience is required; maturity is needed.

Most importantly, it starts in our prayer life, and everything begins in the spiritual realm. God is Spirit; therefore, everything starts in the spiritual first (Jon. 4:24). The text goes on to say we then long for the redemption of our bodies; we long to be released from the body to come fully home. That is what the Holy Spirit within long for in prayer in our hearts. Longing for us to be in God's house: the Father, the Son, and the Holy Spirit. Longing to be connected, intertwined with all parts of God, longing to know everything about Him, for, by this, we come to yearn for being able to be pleasing to Him. And yet, at the same time, we long to come fully home to be with Him. That's why we long for the second coming of Christ. That should be a natural consequence of having a great prayer life, an enjoyable, joyous, and marvelous time with Christ, and the cravings for the promises of Christ. That which longs within us is our spirit so that our soul: emotions, thoughts, and will, come into alignment with God's will. It is still the workings of the Holy Spirit within, enabling us to surrender our lives, our faculties to Him.

> *For in [this] hope we were saved. But hope [the object of] which is seen is not hope. For how can one hope for what he already sees? (Romans 8:24)*

God longs to see us live and move in hope through our prayer life, shaping our whole life. Our salvation is the pathway for the hope to be fulfilled. Looking at the Hebrew word hope, we find the obvious matter: confidence, pleasure, and faith. These faculties come to life within us; His Spirit provides this confidence.

> *Now faith is the assurance (the confirmation, the title deed) of the things [we] hope for, being the proof of things [we] do not see and the conviction of their reality [faith perceiving as real fact what is not revealed to the senses]. (Hebrew 11:1)*

He has given us the enjoyable part for us to do it through Him: Him working within us, making us realize we are unable. This is the enjoyable part for us to learn that if we stop striving, we get to enjoy. It becomes pleasurable for us to walk with God. When we are hoping, we are moved to walk in faith. Hope makes us walk in faith; hope is the assurance of the faith provided. By this, we stop looking into the world for answers in all things, but we focus our full attention on Him, out walking our faith, circumstance by circumstance. We understand that all affairs in life can only be fully solved in Christ because we must always consider the affairs of the adversary working in the activities of the world. We are not fighting against flesh and blood, which moves in the physical world, but against spiritual powers in the heavenly realms. We can't trust what we see in the world, but we can trust God; in our prayer life, that is the unseen path, the dark walk of the soul, and that is the faith walk He longs for us to walk in. In our prayer life, we walk by faith in the darkness and use our faith to walk with Him. We don't lean on or attach ourselves to visions, apprehensions, and revelations; we walk by faith to search out Christ in everything.

> *But if we hope for what is still unseen by us, we wait for it with patience and composure. (Romans 8:25)*

In the waiting period, patience and composure are maturing, all growing into the spiritually mature person He has in store for us to become. As one clearly can see, this is not something we can do. We can only stay at ease in troubled times in Him, and likewise in the good times; it is, in fact, very easy for the foot to slip away from our path in the good times. In the hard times, it's easy for us to cry out to God; this arises naturally. We must realize that we need to shout even more in the good times because we are so easily led astray by things of the world. Hence the language of the world speaks to our emotions. Staying fresh and anew before God by constantly leaning onto, cleaving to, and relying on Him, enables us not to fall spiritually asleep so that we are being led away by going back to the carnal man's conformity of the ways of life. Reaching that we don't carry the trait of any spiritual life given matters, we submit, go low, wait and yield before Him. By this, our lives are transformed, sanctified, and matured.

This requires we give Him our time. That is one of the main issues regarding having a deep-rooted prayer life, giving Him our schedule of life.

> *So too the [Holy] Spirit comes to our aid and bears us up in our weakness; for we do not know what prayer to offer nor how to offer it worthily as we ought, but the Spirit Himself goes to meet our supplication and pleads in our behalf with unspeakable yearnings and groaning's too deep for utterance. (Romans 8:26)*

That means that the Holy Spirit, which is not bound by anything, lifts our soul: our emotions, thoughts, and body, into alignment with the Spirit and, by this, transforms us into the new creation, sanctifying us. He lifts us up, and we are released from things that are bound in the physical. His Spirit is lifting our souls up into the alignment of His truth. A spiritual merging takes place. We receive revelation and transformation through the purgation of the Holy Spirit within us. But still, it is a mystery how. Seemingly in the same manner when Jesus was being raised in the tomb. How did God do that? We don't know; only God knows.

In prayer, there are three things I want to take out:

1. There is a nullification of the emotion. All disturbances of emotions stop. One could almost call it a release from emotions.

2. There is the part when the emotions align with God's will. Our old man's life and emotions die, and we get to live in the new creation in Christ. Therefore, we receive new thoughts and new emotions. The thoughts and emotions of Christ are very different from the nature of the carnal man. They are incomparable.

3. There is the part where His Spirit and ours become one, and we are being lifted up and merged and sometimes raptured.

When we experience our walk with Christ in this matter, we come to know and live an inseparable life with Christ. During prayer, when the Holy Spirit has taken over, it is no longer us in any effort, but we grasp that we are making ourselves available. Because of that openness and availability, the Holy Spirit can move through us and do the whole work. Through being available, waiting, and loving on Him, we are being lifted to that heavenly place: the Third Heaven. In our soul: in us, we do not know how to offer, meaning we don't have the spiritual ability how to present it worthy enough before God. The Holy Spirit comes and lifts our prayer and makes it worthy to present it before the throne of God, which makes it worthy to the Father.

Thus, the Spirit hears our prayer because it is Jesus Spirit interceding before God: hearing our supplication, our groaning, our mourning, our everything, and it is the Holy Spirit doing the groaning in and through us - and take it, lifts it and presents it before the Father. Our life has been surrendered to Christ; therefore, it is no longer the desires of our carnal man's prayer that are being prayed. The prayers of the plan from the Father are now being prayed in for our lives. The purpose He had planned for our lives before the creation of the world is being prayed into existence: His desires for our lives. The Holy Spirit, which is the Spirit of Jesus, is pleading on our behalf. He is on His knees; Jesus is on His knees for us. He already did it and is doing it in the spiritual again. He is interceding for us, yearning and groaning with deep utterance.

The Holy Spirit reveals the realities of eternal life, and because of that, we experience heaven in eternal life right then because our mind is pre-wired for these revelations. God created us to live a spiritually connected life with Him: out of love for us. He does not want us to be distant. Therefore, it is no longer a mystery; now, it becomes the open door and us entering God's throne room. This is not something He wanted to be difficult or hard for us because He loves us.

The reason for us to be able to see in the heavenly realms is that our spirit is merged with His in the heavenly place; we get to be here on earth physically and yet, at the same time, be able to see and be in the heavenly place. That is what enables us to experience the spiritual part of God. When we are in that place in the spirit, we can receive a revelation of Him, His plans, His kingdom, and so on because He keeps pouring out His revelations to us. All of this is birthed out of the waiting and listening on Him. We must wait. Don't rush in the spirit, be in the spirit. Listen. Wait. Yield. What happens is this: the soul gets in this laid-back position where the Spirit can take over and, at some point, lift us up, take us out of our physical body and merge with the Spirit. The relief of being freed from oneself is the most wonderful thing ever. We are being freed from emotions, body, own thinking, own ways, and we enter into His ways, His thought, and His ways of walking through life here on earth. It is such a relief to be able to walk in His footsteps. He made it so easy; we have to come to Him and give our time to Him. We present ourselves to Him and give our time to Him. That's all we do, and we wait.

In the waiting, we wait. He knows what's on our hearts and what's in our lives. God knows everything. We don't have to say anything, and the more we become aware that He knows, the faster the solutions come to our problems because we don't interfere – we wait.

It is a faith walk in the spiritual, and this is what prayer should be. It's the opposite with Him, the world tells us we need to do before we can receive, but with Him, that is an interference. We are in that walking in faith, in the spirit realm, which enables the spiritual to manifest in the physical.

> *And He Who searches the hearts of men knows what is in the mind of the [Holy] Spirit [what His intent is] because the Spirit intercedes and pleads [before God] on behalf of the saints according to and in harmony with God's will. (Romans 8:27)*

The Holy Spirit lifts us up into the intention of the plan of the Father. The Holy Spirit is interceding for us for these plans to come to pass. The Holy Spirit comes on the inner and lifts us up, and we go to the Throne Room before God. The Holy Spirit knows what is in our hearts, and He searches our hearts out; what is He searching for? What we need in us to align with God's will. He is purging our souls in every way so that the will of God can be fulfilled in our lives. He is aligning our spiritual life, physical life, and soulish life into God's plan - in God's will.

By this, everything in the spiritual becomes logical, and the supernatural becomes natural. We no longer wonder about anything in the spiritual because we sense very quickly right from wrong. It doesn't mean we know why, but we just know; hence we are being led by the Holy Spirit. We come to live out the fact that it has nothing to do with us, but it has everything to do with Jesus. An important remark is that God's plans for lives are so good for us to comprehend. That's why we have to know the will of God. Otherwise, we might miss out on the plans He has for our life because the way the Lord leads us is always an unknown way from what we could ever imagine or comprehend. God's plans for mankind are unimaginable good. That is why we must know what His plans are for the whole body of Christ and thus mankind, enabling us to support each person He has positioned in His kingdom. All in all, we should not interfere out of opinion but support each person in their calling.

*Elena Radef*

# Chapter 15

# What are Intercessory Prayers

**The understanding and importance of intercessory prayer**

There is a lot of misconception about the whole area of intercessory prayer. Most people think that they are the ones standing in the gap when they are in prayer for someone. We are not standing in the gap when we are in intercessory prayer. That is what the prophets did in the Old Testament, and notice that they were still only able to pray for some, not for all, to have a repenting heart. All people in the Old Testament could only fulfill a task for a period of time, and only in some areas in the gifting to show us we need a Savior. One who could complete all office positions; to give Himself away for all of mankind to lead us individually in our lives. And that requires a Spirit that is omnipotent and almighty like God. Nobody could fulfill that position but Jesus, and out of this, He could do it for all of mankind in a one-time event. Everything in the Old Testament is a foreshadowing of what Jesus was going to fulfill. The prophets were instruments God chose to use to fulfill the task for a certain period, time, or group, but only Jesus could fulfill the whole task for mankind through a one-time occurrence: the Cross. The standing in gap position was always meant to be a position for Christ and for us to see that only He could fulfill it, all to confess the need for a Savior, returning our hearts to Him, in that returning home. We know now that Jesus fulfilled His calling here on earth, and because of that, He is now the one standing in the gap for us.

Intercessory prayer is us seeking the face of God on behalf of people, nations, problems, or difficult circumstances in life, that have become a burden laid upon us by the Spirit. The Spirit needs someone to pray through, it needs someone to pour its heart out through, it needs a vessel, and we are that vessel the Spirit chooses to use. The Holy Spirit fills people through a burdensome prayer and prays through them. God longs for everyone, every situation, and every nation to be filled with His glory because He loves us so much (Joh. 3:16). He longs so much for all His children on the earth to know Him and walk with Him. When Christ died on The Cross, in that He took the place for us – that's the same thing we do when we are interceding, we carry the burden.

There are two kinds of movements of the Spirit within us in intercessory prayer, and two kinds of expressions:

1. We are taking their place; we are covering up, just as Jesus covered up for us on the Cross by taking our sins. That sometimes involves that we carry their tribulations, whether emotional, physical, or spiritual, as a weight laid upon us. This consists of a trial or burdensome weight being removed from a person, group, or nation that is placed upon us and that we carry silently. The prime example of this is what Jesus did on the Cross. Jesus fulfilled the task completely, yet we undergo the same for others on a minor scale. This could also be done through fasting and or hours of praying.

2. Here, we are the ones whom the Holy Spirit uses as a vessel to cry and long. Often, it involves physical crying. We are the ones crying on behalf of that person, nation, or group; for them to repent and turn their heart toward Christ. The Spirit of Jesus expresses Himself through us, through crying and outward groanings. This is what one could call the spiritual and emotional burdensome prayer. Jesus' resurrecting Lazarus back to life event is of such matter (Joh. 11: 1-44).

And, of course, we can experience both in intercessory prayer for others, at the same time and individually. Everything we do, we do it in and through Christ – He did it for us on the Cross first, and through that, it enabled us to do it, which is why the Cross is the most important historic thing that has ever happened. This is also why we outlive the happening of the Cross over and over in our lives. What He did on the Cross for us, we are outliving through our lives in the circumstances we undergo. We die and come to life in every situation in our life. In both cases of intercessory prayer, we experience the following; when we are interceding, we are being used by the Holy Spirit to lift that person, group, or nation to Father God's attention through Christ. The Holy Spirit within us pours out the cry and is using us to ask in prayer: Father, help them. In that, we don't ask by words; it merely becomes an outcry of the heart through praying in tongues or carrying the burden, so utterance of groanings comes to life. We might receive some revelation in what we are praying about, but we might not know how because it is the Holy Spirit who has taken over. That could seem like a mystery to many because the Holy Spirit takes over bodily as well. We might find ourselves crying and being deeply touched in a way that we don't recognize ourselves, or we even get the sense of being alienated from ourselves and in life. One could say we lose ourselves in prayer. What happens in intercessory prayer is that it becomes an expression of longing, the outcry of the Holy Spirit who longs for His children. Jesus is the door to the Father, and He uses us to call His children in through the groanings and crying. We see this displayed among others in the Old Testament with the prophet Elijah:

> *So Ahab went up to eat and to drink. And Elijah went up to the top of Carmel; and he bowed himself down upon the earth and put his face between his knees (1 Kings 18:42)*

First, he went up upon the mount Carmel, which is a spiritual state for us to come into the place of intercessory prayer. Moses, Abraham, and Jesus also went to the mountain to pray. A place reached of such dept, depicted as height, where one comes into a union with the Holy Spirit that nothing else can take place other than prayer. The same we see displayed with Christ in the New Testament when He raises Lazarus from the dead. In the Gospel of John, we see the works of intercessory prayer moving through Christ (Joh. 11:33, 35,38). In the physical part of intercessory prayer, there is movement. God is God of movement; therefore, when the Spirit is in action within, it moves our physical body.

Consequently, we might find ourselves on our knees, laying down, going back and forth, finding ourselves in unknown positions, and often alone. It is a prayer between us and the Lord for that person, group, or nation. We don't want interferences. We want to be led by the Spirit; a deep grief is upon us, and all we can bear is to be with the Lord.

We don't want the pity of others because they think we are sad. Therefore, most often, we withdraw. Also, the Lord puts it on us when we are by ourselves; He wants to lead us. Jesus often withdrew to be in prayer (Luk. 5:16, 6:12-13, 22:39-44, Matt. 14:23).

This is only something God can do in us because it is only Him who knows what prayer is needed. We must never come to a point to think that we know what the problem is and how it should be solved because we don't know what has happened in people's lives, their situations, etc. Even if the Lord chooses to show us, we must never become confident that we know. We should merely try to remain open instead of certain; openness instead of certainty is the garment of character we aim for, all for the devil not to get any foothold in us and stay humble. Certainty can bring the carnal man into a position of knowledge, and often out of that grows pride. That's why openness is a better garment to wear.

> *We are assured and know that [God being a partner in their labor] all things work together and are (fitting into a plan] for good to and for those who love God and are called according to [His] design and purpose. For those whom He foreknew [of whom He was aware and loved beforehand], He also destined form the beginning [foreordaining them] to be molded into the image of His Son [and share inwardly His likeness], that He might become the firstborn among many brethren. (Romans 8:28-29)*

Before the beginning of time, the nature of prayer was in God, just as it is now. It is a trademark of God, and we are exposed to it in our conversion. In our acceptance of Him, we give ourselves to the Lord as a vessel through which He can pour His Spirit. Deep-founded prayer life must be founded on the Cornerstone Who was the inventor of it: the Trinity of God. Hence Jesus Christ is the only living God. We must know that for a prayer to come to life, and it must go through Him. Dead things like wood and stone cannot give life, yet many believe for it to be so, sadly. The reason for this occurrence is because of the weakness in the church, in not living a proper and healthy prayer life; the intimate communing prayer life with the Lord. He loved us before we were born; that means everything is birthed from prayer. Who prayed for us before we got saved, Jesus, and Who prayed that we should be saved, Jesus. He knew us before we were born: before I formed you, I knew you (Jer. 1:5). Jesus is praying for us in heaven (Rom. 8:26), which means we don't have the ability to know how to pray; it is the Holy Spirit praying through us. He prayed for us before we were born when God created us.

> *Who is there to condemn [us]? Will Christ Jesus (the Messiah), Who died, or rather Who was raised from the dead, Who is at the right hand of God actually pleading as He intercedes for us? (Romans 8:34)*

Therefore, we can intercede on behalf of others now that we know that it is not us praying but the Holy Spirit praying through us.

To pray in Hebrew means: intervene, interpose, make favorable judgment, expected, intercede, intersession, to ask for, to make a request of a court. And that is precisely what the Holy Spirit is doing through us, and after the prayer has been poured out through us, the prayers ascend before the Father. As a beautiful fragrance that is pleasing to Him. In the knowledge that the Holy Spirit is the Spirit of Jesus, we see that it is Jesus coming before the Father with the Holy prayers. They are Holy because they come from His Spirit, and that is the prayers the Father can give heed to. The Father is so Divine and Holy that the only thing that can come near Him is likewise Holy and Divine. Nobody else could offer such Holy prayers except the Spirit of Jesus because He offered Himself as a well-pleasing sacrifice first. In that, He did what the Father asked of Him, which is why the Father responds to the request to the Spirit of Jesus, the Holy Spirit.

*Elena Radef*

# Chapter 16

# Growing in the Intimate Relationship with God

**Song of Solomon: a love story**

The best songs we learn to sing before Christ is the worship needed for spiritual growth and the constant renewal and ongoing of His love in us to reach more profound heights and depths. Therefore, we sing our best song to Him; our best one always becomes the new one; hence we are in constant growth in His love, which Song of Solomon means; the best song. The love story in Song of Solomon has three main themes: the allegorical part about God and Israel. The literal perspective, God's teachings on love and marriage, and the typical interpretation about Jesus and the church. In the narrowing down between Jesus and the church, the attention is to be moved toward how to grow in virtue in relation to God. Virtue, in this sense, is of the power and strength, the tenderness and sweet loving-kindness, and the moving and dynamic force of God. In other words, being filled and led by the Holy Spirit, living a surrendered life in Christ, abandoned life from the world, and being purged in His presence.

Which is the part I want to address from the Song of Solomon; the intimacy in the relationship translated into our prayer life and daily walk and living with God Jesus. This is the relationship we need to have and seek out; an intimate prayer life with Jesus. Our personal relationship with Him is the most important place for us to live, be and constantly grow in, deeper and deeper. One could argue that the signs of His presence would be the signs, wonders, and miracles, but we see in scripture that this is not so, and on many occasions, I have found it to be so. The only thing we should focus on is growing in His love. Out of this flows the attributes of life into others areas: signs, wonders, and miracles. However, that is not our primary focus. Our growing in His love and staying close to Him is our only security because we are on the small path of life with Christ. The devil can perform too, and far too many are performing signs, wonders, and miracles in the name of the adversary without their knowledge:

> *Not everyone who says to Me, Lord, Lord, will enter the kingdom of heaven, but he who does the will of My Father Who is in heaven. Many will say to Me in that day, Lord, Lord, have we not prophesied in Your name, and driven out demons in Your name, and done many mighty works in Your name? And then I will say to them openly (publicly), I never knew you; depart from Me, you who act wickedly [disregarding My commands]. (Matthew 7:21-23)*

The Great Commandment and thus Commission to perform is the love of Christ; we must know that everything flows from the love of Christ Jesus; this is our run, aim, and goal in all:

> *And He replied to him, you shall love the Lord your God with all your heart and with all your soul and with all your mind (intellect). This is the great (most important, principal) and first commandment. (Matthew. 22:37-38)*

Loving God means that we follow His commandments; that we do them; we stay alert to them; we watch over them; we protect them; we keep them dear to us; we long for them, and they become our most valuable treasure:

> *For the [true] love of God is this: that we do His commands [keep His ordinances and are mindful of His precepts and teaching]. And these orders of His are not irksome (burdensome, oppressive, or grievous). (1 John 5:3)*

It is a lost path of the Christian life. We look at His hands and power instead of Him. Out of that grows a Christianity, in which the love of Christ is not present, but a carnal search and interpretation of Christ have taken over. Again, reference to that point (Matt. 7: 21-23). Jesus longs for us to walk and live in the inheritance He has provided for us, but we must first be purged before we can handle the power of the inheritance. Until that, He can't trust us with the influence He longs to provide to us. We are so fickle; hence it would be dangerous for us if He did. The carnal man can't handle power; only through Christ within we can handle power. Through the walking and waiting on Him, we come to fully understand that it is not us who have or carry any power. He makes this point to us through that one big issue we have tried exceedingly hard to solve in our life. We all have at least one big issue that we can't seem to get around no matter how hard we try. God allows this to occur so that we may know for sure, in a revelatory and personal way, through the spiritual fact that we cannot perform or have any power. He is teaching us humbleness, and when we learn to be humble through purgation, only then can we become useful for the power of God. The degree of humility we are being purged through equals the degree of power that can be moved through us.

Another point to consider regarding the carnal man's weakness is how Satan deceives people in this area. He appeals to the carnal man's unprocessed emotions, mind, and will. The easiest way to manipulate people is to make them think that they are more and better, even just slightly better than others. He is deceiving them to believe that they have the power. This way of thinking is the foundation of the heart of Satan. He moves in the opposite direction than God, moving away from humbleness, and instead, he turns up the volume of pride. This occurs a little at a time, always voicing out pride through the justification of exceptionalism. With the weakness of the carnal combined with how the devil uses it, we apprehend why the Lord is purging us for such a long time so that we won't fall into deception of any kind. It is always a matter of returning to the heart of Christ; returning to the love of Jesus Christ, that is our mightiest weapon. Therefore, we must seek out the means and matters of the heart of Christ. What is on the heart of the Lord, how did Jesus walk on earth, what did He do, and why? We must, by all means, seek to find out an intimate loving relationship with Christ Jesus. That Jesus, He is our beloved, in the sense of how it is described in the Song of Solomon. The picture of a woman and a man is of Jesus and us in an intimate relationship where we get to know Him and His deepest desires and longings. We are searching Him out, discovering who He is in every sense. Hence we want to know everything about Him out of love for Him. There is a mystery in this because somehow, it also seems that He is searching us out in prayer. This is experienced through His love for us. When we are in love, we always seem to search for a deeper place within our spouse, all in order to come closer. The love of Christ is searching us out, unfolding more and more of Himself at a pace we can handle, enabling us to abide deeper and deeper in His love, all in order to come closer (1 Cor. 2:9-10). When we are intimate with Jesus, as described in the Song of Solomon, we get this deep desire to know Him so well. A place where Jesus is sitting down and having communion with us one-on-one; in that He is exposing everything of Himself to us because He wants us to trust Him. Through this, we lose track of everything else in life, and the world becomes tasteless because we experience, see and perceive that He is all. The inner place of communion and sacrament is Him exposing everything of Himself. Because of Him doing so, we forget our own life's self-importance, losing ourselves in the loving arms of Christ. A death of surety takes place without our knowledge. We learn to trust the security that He provides, something we in the carnal never can comprehend because the carnal does not understand the ways of the Lord.

It is a secret place because it occurs between two lovers of spirit, something that only they know about. An understanding that only they can fathom. It is something so beautiful that they want to keep it a secret. Secrets are likewise hard to divulge or convey, implying a special place of belonging we have never experienced before. This love affair is not something that passes; it keeps merging deeper. Our life becomes a confession before Christ; all our actions and thoughts hold the awareness of confession. An awareness we receive through the Holy Spirit. A condition where we become keenly aware of our life's movement; in all aspects of being a human. The rising knowledge in His presence exposes all sides of ourselves.

Agape love is where two lovers speak a language only they can speak; they understand each other in a beautifully poetic way. This is depicted so eloquently in Songs of Solomon. One needs to unpack the words and the pictorial story to comprehend the true meaning of heart in it. One cannot grasp it with one's mind: one must take the heart to help reveal the affair of love. One can never fathom matters of love with the mind. The mind is used to observe the condition of the heart and thus word it. The working of love takes place in the heart. We realize His omnipresence combined with His love for us, and by this, we come into a dependent relationship with Him. We come to understand that if we're not following His leadership, that will create the possibility of losing the closeness with Him. Consequently, it forms a dependent trust on Him; the dying into His arms, the surrender comes alive. All because we come to know how much He loves us.

**The Chase**

In reading Song of Solomon, one experiences the chase between two lovers. The first pursuit is Him searching for her, and when she tastes His passion for her, that ignites her passion for Him, a chase where she pursues Him. A chase has much to do with not being far from each other because one feeds on the love in the relationship. She is the one being fed as in searching for Him. He is describing her growing qualities, which He sees are blossoming in her. Take notice that when the Lord speaks, there is life, which leads to the importance of them declaring their love for one another. This is the declaration that needs to be spoken. Every time He purposely draws away, she becomes more hungry for what He offers. It is not to become Him but to become the love He offers, which she experiences. In her transformation in search for Him, in losing herself, dying to herself where she no longer cares about what others might think, she is molded into what He offers, the pure intimate close love. In this, she is no longer away from Him, and she is no longer searching for Him because now she has become what she searched for, love. Now, she has merged with the love and is also purged from her way in the love relationship. Her old ways and life are now transformed into new ways and life through the love He gave her. Now, she is at home in Him, depicted by how they are merged in the end.

Now, they are a match because she is no longer what she was. Out of this, He is describing her more and more eloquently and detailed because she is transformed and purged. All description has to do with all the faculties of the soul being merged, and He is describing them by name-calling them: He sees all.

When He tells her, she is in them, shown what she has been purged from. All beauty comes out, shown when she is being purged, which has to do with her chase for Him and her passion for Him.

In the chase for Him, one loses the behavior of the carnal man through forgetfulness of how to live the old life, which is the whole purpose of a chase of love for Christ because the new life with Christ is so lovely. In this matter, one dies to the old ways and lifestyle. In the chase for Christ, we die, and in the occupation for Him, we hardly notice on the inside how His love kills, purges, and transforms us. Contrary to the outer physical circumstances, they can be very rough to go through. We might not understand their workings regarding the heart's purgation and transformation, yet all are needed. Otherwise, we will find no occurrence of the purgation.

That is the love affair, and in the end, we have died, and the only survivor is Christ within us.

We discover what it means to have a healthy inner relationship in this secret place.

This love affair is not something that passes; it keeps getting deeper and deeper. We grow deeper and deeper into this relationship – it is a never-ending one. In this relationship, we long to tell Him everything. We come to a point where we don't just want to talk about the good and nice things, and we don't just want Him to smooth talk us. Still, we want to show Him all our bad stuff, our ugly stuff, our faults, and the things we say or do that are off. We want to be corrected because we long to come closer and closer, just like we experience it when we are in a relationship with someone we love – we want them to know everything, just like we long to know everything about them. It is depicted in this way for us to grasp in the spiritual what agape love is. It is a deep longing to be close to that person – in this case, Jesus, and it is depicted so eloquently in the Song of Solomon. The longing for us to be close to Him is also where we realize His omnipotence, combined with His love for us; we come into a dependent relationship with Him. Therefore, we seek His guidance, so we don't lose

## Chapter 16: Growing in the Intimate Relationship with God

the closeness with Him. We come to understand if we don't follow His leadership in our lives, the possibility of losing the closeness becomes a reality. And because of that, we come into a dependent trust in Him; the dying into His arms; the surrender takes place, all because we come to know how much He loves us. We come to realize that He is the only one who can set things straight in our lives; regarding past events, in the ones we are in, and in the ones to come. We grasp that the influence of our life here on earth, walking with the Lord, has a direct consequence and effect in the afterlife. Therefore, we want to do our best not to let the future part of our lives become so influenced by the past that we must take detours over and over. Still, instead, we want to grow deeper and deeper, instead of going around the mountain again and again. This is the introduction to Song of Solomon. Now we are going deeper into the scripture of what it means regarding the intimate relationship.

Let me also say that the purgation and the scripture regarding the purgation are not all chronological. However, the different processes we all must undergo in our purgation.

Only a few verses are full in context. So follow along in your Bible.

The explanation is as follows; whenever she and we are written, that should be thought about ourselves. Therefore, using "Him" or "He" refers to Jesus in relation to us.

The allegory in this scripture we have to take notice of is how Jesus is disguised as a shepherd but, in reality, is a King. The same takes place in the story; Solomon is a King but disguised himself as a shepherd to win her love because of her lower rank position in life. It would be impossible for him to win her over as a king because she could never commit to that because of her lower social status. At that time, a King could not marry a common. So, he strips himself off to win her love. Jesus stripped Himself of His royalty to become low, to be able to come and redeem us. This process of inner redemption occurs over and over in our prayer life. The purgation and sanctification process is happening over and over within for us to be redeemed in every area of our life.

Please notice for further enhancement of words. See appendix.

(Sg. 1:1-4) We see the first meeting with our Lord, our salvation. She meets Him, and she describes His beauty in every way. She recognizes He is the answer for her love and inner restoration. We also understand that He is our answer to our inner calling. She is already describing the wondrous of His attributes because the sweetness of His touch in our salvation makes us recognize the peace and life there is within. She brings it forth by describing Him. Spiritually, the occurrence is the inner exchange that takes place the instant we say yes. There is an immediate shift away that changes everything on the inside; the Holy Spirit is moving in and fills us with life, and out goes death and decay that follows the life of the carnal man. In that instant, the touch of His anointing has been bestowed upon our lives; *The odor of your ointment is fragrant* (Sg.1:3). The new creation within is experienced; *your name is like perfume poured out* (Sg.1:3). Even though this takes place, it is not a finished work. We must know that purgation and transformation must still be experienced to not lose the Holy Spirit.

We also come to fathom the love people, the church, have for the Lord. Through this, we come to care for each other, as was the Lord's intention; *Therefore, do the maidens love you* (Sg.1:3). Only through charity the church stands strong and can continue to stand. This matter is important for us to receive as quickly as possible; that the Lord provides charity to us through salvation in a way that we would want to find a place, a home, in the church. This necessity is immediate because, without the protection of the church, we won't be able to stand.

> *[And she continues] The odor of your ointments is fragrant; your name is like perfume poured out. Therefore do the maidens love you. (Song of Solomon 1:3)*

(Sg. 1:5) She recognizes His beauty; she sees what she lacks; *I am so black* (Sg. 1:5). She sees her sinful nature; in prayer, it means that the Lord points to attitudes, emotions, and all soulish nature; lust, cravings, desires, impurities, indecency, and immorality. (Gal. 5:19-21) talks about the doings, and practices, of the flesh. In this matter, the Lord will point to them in prayer, and He will purge us from them, and He will eventually renounce them when we come into the depth of the knowledge by heart that we cannot change, alter, submit, or let go of any of them ourselves. He renounced them all on the Cross, the ultimate liberation. Therefore, we can come to live a life of liberation. However, we cannot contain more than one step at a time.

Consequently, we receive liberation in Christ Jesus one step at a time, knowing He has already liberated us. Through each step, the spiritual realization of liberation brings forth the life He provided for us. This sounds like a mystery, but it is not a mystery on the path of purgation. However, one can only fathom these affairs by walking through the fire of purgation.

Some seeming contradictions in the operating and workings of the Holy Spirit will occur but still, spiritually, all point to the same truth.

(Sg. 1:6) She has tried very hard to fix her own life; *[Please] do not look at me, [she said, for] I am swarthy [I have worked out] in the sun and it has left its mark upon me* (Sg. 1:6). She has not kept her own vineyard but kept the others that her stepbrothers told her to do, meaning everything in life gets the wrong priority. She recognizes her own inadequacy to do things right, to live a righteous and purposeful life that brings meaning on every level. This we come to realize in our life.

In communion prayer, this understanding by heart provides the fullness of what the life lived with Christ brings; a meaning and synthesis where everything in us emerges and comes into alignment; that's the picture of the love relationship described.

(Sg. 1:7) She recognizes the beauty of His love and what it does to her; how it makes her feel to be loved by His love; here we see her returning her love to Him; *O you whom my soul loves* (Sg.1:7).

It is important to express love, and we cannot help ourselves not doing so because love is alive and moving. Thus, it makes us understand by heart from whom this love derives; we know for sure that we cannot produce such love; it is simply not within. Only by being with Him do we understand by heart that He is the reason, the way, the truth, and the life. We see fully in the reflection of His face how much we do not carry these love traits. She sees the rest, peace, and care He has for His sheep; she recognizes that she needs to learn to rest and that He longs for her to rest and be in peace. This is what Jesus is teaching us in His presence; that only through rest do we produce fruit. In the purgation, we die to strive and work and step into peace and rest; we come to understand that only through peace there is power. We come to know how contrary everything is with the Lord when we think of power and strength through the ways of the world, which is power in the terminology of God equals peace (Psa. 23).

> *If you do not know [where your lover is], O you fairest among women, run along, follow the tracks of the flock, and [amuse yourself by] pasturing your kids beside the shepherds' tents. (Songs of Solomon 1:8)*

(Sg. 1:8) Sometimes we lose sight of the Lord: *If you do not know* (Sg.1:8), then we must seek back to the guidance of the steps: *follow the tracks of the flocks* (Sg.1:8) that will return us into the close intimate relationship with Him. We must nurture/search out; *[amuse yourself by]* (Sg.1:8) that within which makes us unable to lose sight of Him, which often has to do with an immature spiritual hindrance within; *pasturing your kids* (Sg.1:8). When we're together with kids, we need time, patience, and waiting. The kids here resemble immature emotions that have not been turned over to and purged by Christ. In prayer, when we are drawn away from the closeness with Him, we must do and act the same as when we are with children: yield, patience, and wait, which brings us back to Christ. Sometimes we must turn to others under the attention of someone who has walked the path before us. Now, this is also about looking at how the ministers of God attended to our situation; this would involve reading the Bible and sometimes turning to an overseer in our lives; *beside the shepherds' tents* (Sg. 1:8).

(Sg. 1: 9) He loves on us; *O my love [he said as he saw her]* (Sg. 1:9), which in the Hebrew language has a double meaning here because it also means tend my flock, in meaning; we are now ready to pour out the love on people, the flock. The beauty of a horse has to do with the controlled strength and grace in which a horse moves when it is steered through training by the reins, which resembles us being under the guidance of Him, purging us, and steering our lives in the right direction. The horses of Pharaoh were the most expensive ones; it is that which is expensive in our lives, something that costs us the highest price to receive that which Jesus has in store for us; we pay with our very own life; all included from this life. And the beauty of this in the eyes of the Lord is that we become to look so beautiful, like a young mare; which is also the only place where we can run our race in strength; hence we only have strength through Him.

> *Your cheeks are comely with ornaments, your neck with strings of jewels. We will make for your chains and of gold, studded with silver. (Song of Solomon 1:10-11)*

The beauty we start to show is depicted as the jewelry; the beauty is His glory shining forth within and showing on the outer appearance. In verse 11, we see the three persons in the Godhead: *We will make* (Sg.1:11), the Trinity, meaning that it is all of God shaping us and leading us along. The Holy Spirit to abide within and guide us, The Father upholding the plan, and Jesus as the mediator. We are having communion with Christ in prayer, *While the king sits at his table* (Sg. 1:12). It is His table because He was the one providing the atonement, and only He can defeat the enemies that try to defeat us (Psa. 23). In the story of the rich women and Elisha (2 Kgs 4:9-10), we see the allegory displayed in the same manner, and by this, we also come to understand that it is only He who can set the table; therefore, it is His table. Through communion, anointing can flow: *sends forth [His] fragrances* (Sg. 1:12).

(Sg. 1:13) Jesus is now so becoming to us He; becomes our most precious life: bosom: heart. His presence is our very own life; *it is to me like a [scent] bag of myrrh that lies in my bosom* (Sg. 1:13); therefore, our life becomes precious. This includes everything in life and by this life on earth. The earth is very dear to Him, and He loves the world; *for God so loved the world* (Joh. 3:16). This scripture becomes alive in us. He came to save what He holds dear to Him, and what is most precious to Him is us. Through this, we receive spiritually all He did for us: The Cross. Only through the right spiritual, biblical understanding can we receive it, which will allow the flow from the inner fountain, the anointing of Christ Jesus. We must understand that the devil has his anointing (Job 41:31-32). It describes here that at a distance, it looks like anointing. The distance resembles the lack of spiritual discernment; because of that, one could think that it is the Holy Spirit. If not discerning right, one can easily discern wrongly and mistakenly think that the devil's anointing is God's. To discern rightly, one must spend time with the Lord and read His Word. The analogy is as follows; if we want to know what pure gold is like, we must study pure gold. We cannot study semi-pure gold and think we receive an understanding of pure gold; all we receive is wrong information, and we are thereby being deceived. Many people behave in this manner regarding the anointing, receiving second-hand information, and taking it for granted to be true. We must go through all affairs, study, and pray to know Him.

(Sg. 1:14) He is all life to us; we understand by Him only provision is completed in the right timing of all things in our life. *En-Gedi* is a pleasant and well-watered place; therefore, enriched by all living things to live a good and pleasant life. I do want to emphasize that this refers to the inner riches of Christ Jesus. There is a blessing in life that follows when we are abiding within Christ Jesus; it is a natural spiritual consequence of walking with Him. Hence everything is His. He loves us, therefore, gives/provides, but there has and still is way too much focus on what the Lord can bring into our lives, looking at His hands, compared to keeping our focus on what is the most important thing, which is the love of Christ Jesus, referred here as the riches of God. Which are the true riches of life; *But seek (aim at and strive after) first of all His Kingdom and His righteousness (His way of doing and being right), and then all these things taken together will be given you besides (Matt. chapter 6:33).* These all-other things are the ones that Jesus mentions in chapters 5 and 6; that means as a natural consequence of seeking Him first and His way of doing and being right, then everything else will follow. Therefore, He says, if you do like Me; in the knowledge of I have conquered it all for you; then you will receive it all and therefore don't need to worry.

(Sg. 1:15) His beauty springs forth from the knowledge of His dove eyes, innocence, and purity of Christ Jesus. We understand spiritually how He was innocent, that He was a sinless man taking all sin upon Himself to redeem us. We are being moved by His compassion and how perfect, loving, and kind He is. This will start to overflow in our lives; we are now being moved by compassion in our life, touching people's lives by sharing the love of Christ in various ways.

Understanding these things in a revelatory and spiritual way means that we get it through the Holy Spirit within, which means that we, in some spiritual sense, experience it. The degree of how intense this occurs varies a lot, but the fact is that this is what is happening when we receive the revelation that, to some level, we live it. This also explains why some experience deeper and more profound revelations than others and why we cannot say in a specific way; this is the right way to receive revelations from our Lord because they vary a lot, likewise in-depth.

Everything we do in life is sprung forth from intimate prayer life with Christ Jesus. In prayer, Jesus shapes us, and we outlive what He has shaped in prayer, which is why we must understand how important it is to spend time in prayer.

(Sg. 1:16) Spiritually, there are always new beginnings in our walk with the Lord; always new areas in our life that need to be given over to Him, more depth, hence new beginnings, which makes us more prosperous and flourishing in all areas of life; *Our arbor and couch are green and leafy* (Sg. 1:16). The color green resembles salvation; with every step taken in Christ through our purgation, there is a constant salvation that takes place; we constantly need to be saved from our old life. The word leaf in Hebrew is taken from the root word *alah*, which means to go up, to ascend, and climb, in reference to going deeper and merging deeper into the intimate relationship, which will eventually happen over time. The Greek word for leaf has derived from the word *phule*, which means tribe or race of people; we come to belong.

> *The beams of our house are cedars, and our rafters and panels are cypresses or pines. (Song of Solomon 1:17)*

The relationship with Christ is strong and lasting: *The beams of our house* (Sg 1:17). Beams will uphold it because it is made of the hardest and most expensive wood, the finest relationship ever, and the most precious one to be held dear in every way. All the best woods resembles the perfect and righteous way of God. Everything the Lord builds is far beyond perfect and whole in every sense and matter.

In chapter 2, we see how we should be pursuing Jesus in our prayer life. It also tells us what we need to pursue.

(Sg. 2:1) His humble nature unfolds within; we are being purged in the deep through difficulties in obstructing the four enemies: the sinful nature, the carnal, the world, and the devil.

In His humbleness and by His humbleness, we become that one lily that sticks out in the plain; now, life becomes for all to see what is life and where life is. The only hope of life exists in Him and through Him; [*that grows in deep and difficult places*] *(Sg. 2:1)*.

(Sg. 2:2) We only become lovely in His eyes when we live a surrendered life in Him; it is the only place where His glory shines and where there is life. The thorns are the daughters of the world, trying to lead us into doing our own thing; by this being wicked. We can only remain a lily in Him when the thorns of life are surrounding us. We then become this beautiful lily among the thorns. Daughters refer to the powers of the world, the devil, the sinful nature and the carnal.

(Sg. 2:3) The only tree that bears fruit is the tree of life, which is Jesus. Trees in the wood do not bear fruit. Fruit trees grow on a plantation, not in a wood, which would make them unable to bear fruit. Fruit trees must stand a certain distance to bear as much fruit as possible. Not all trees bear fruit. Here very clearly stated that the only tree that bears fruit is Jesus; she proclaims His state of being, one fruit tree among trees in the wood. His life stands out. He also differs in personality; *so is my beloved [shepherd] among the sons* (Sg. 2:3), different from all other sons. The only place where we come into the recognition that I need to rest from the strive of the world; thus, the only place of protection is when we come into His presence. We understand by heart how much we need to rest to be able to produce any fruit of life; we come to fathom that we only are in life and become the traits of life through Him. The analogy is to come away from the heat and the sun, which is the pressure of life, which will burn us if not coming under protection will eventually take us out. Then we can experience the lovely tree of life by sitting under it. Also, understanding that only first by this recognition and placement, we are at the starting point of understanding how much we long to sit down, to be at rest. We only come to fathom in this placement what is rest and what is strife. When we live in the world without the Lord, we only think we know what it means to rest, but when we come into His rest, we see that we were never in any rest. Because what Jesus offers is the rest of the Shabbat, which is only to be found in Him. We don't know this until we see His lovely tree; *Under his shadow I delighted to sit* (Sg. 2:3), and the only place for us to being able to eat; *and his fruit was sweet to my taste* (Sg. 2:3). We come to fathom that the food we now eat gives life: by this, we recognize what kind of food the world serves. It can only be recognized by eating real food because it is life-giving and sweet. This is not something we can understand the difference in because this knowledge comes from His Spirit.

Sitting under a tree resembles our heart's position, where it needs to be placed at rest. Only from this point can we move forward and not stumble because our ears are always paying attention to what He is speaking to us. We are invited into deeper communion when we have learned to sit spiritually. We need to learn to rest in our hearts before moving into deeper depths in Him. In other words, it is an absolute necessity. Jesus is our Shabbat, our rest. This place of rest within is what He provided for us, and to move from this point of rest within.

(Sg 2:4) We are also invited into the feast of the church; *He brought me to the banqueting house* (Sg. 2:4). We feast among other fellow brothers and sisters, and Jesus is the King inviting all to the feast, the parable of the wedding feast (Matt. 22:1-14). Here we are being exposed to many different kinds of food, and we learn to feast and eat from the fullness of His table. Spiritually in prayer, this analogy is that we are being exposed to different aspects of the spiritual realm, how to handle what He is exposing us to, what it is, and how to discern. When we eat food, we use our taste buds to discern what we are eating. This analogy is the occurrence of us being exposed to different kinds of food; that means different spiritual events. By this, we learn through the Holy Spirit to discern what is good food and what is poor or bad food. Eating bad or poor food will leave us to become sick or die. This is why we desperately need to learn to discern the happenings of the spiritual realm. That means the Lord will take us through different occurrences in order for us to use those spiritual muscles. Here trials and testing are put before us, but under His banner, we are the land He conquered on the Cross. By this, He has a claim on our lives because He paid with His very own life. The greatest act of love He paid. Therefore, this love banner is waved over our lives; by this, He is saying she is mine to keep. In being near Him, we are comforted by this banner. When we seek refuge in contemplating the Cross, we come to the depths of realization of how much He loves us. Not as a one-time event but as a constant deepening growing intimacy in communion where the revelation keeps unfolding. So, in the times of trials and testing, we are safe.

(Sg. 2:5) The Hebrew word raisin cake has derived from *ashash*, which means to found or establish, and the Hebrew word for apples has derived from the word *naphach*, which means to breathe, blow; more in terms of blowing up. By this, we come to be ignited with His fire and by this eliminating that which was of our old nature. We come to be founded and established and full of His fire of love; His passion and desire for righteousness will burn within. But also, because of this fire, we become more and more lovesick for Him; the never-ending love relationship constantly deepens.

(Sg. 2:6) In this place, we are held in His hands of loving care and nurtured in His protection, held in His arms, and we find relief from the troubles of the world. Holding our skull is the relief we are in need of in our minds. Jesus gave His life on Golgotha, the place of the skull, the one place that needs the utmost attention from us in relation to which thought we are being led by. Are we being led by our thoughts, or are we being led by His thoughts, and only by staying close to Him, with Him holding our heads, are we able to follow and hear His thoughts. We all know the importance of what one thought can lead to. It either leads to life, Jesus, or it leads to death. We need to pay attention to four influences: the devil, the world, the carnal (here, the will in terms of being led by desire), and the sinful nature. The most essential to take hold of is the renewing of the mind, which occurs in being close to Him. This is also where the molding takes place. In yielding and soaking, we are being recollected in His presence by placing our whole attention on His face.

(Sg. 2:7) We cannot make this love happen; He is charging us not to use our own will so that we stop striving in ourselves; *O you daughters of Jerusalem* (Sg. 2:7). Changing requires that Jesus is pointing to the things we need to change. To make it happen, He is saying: *I charge you* (Sg. 2:7), referred to as being led by sensitive emotions; *gazelles or by the hinds of the field* (Sg. 2:7). Gazelles and hinds freely follow their instincts; thus, they resemble unpurged emotions. They also easily get distracted from what they are doing; it takes time to win their trust because scarcity is within their nature. This is a direct picture of how our carnal man functions.

So, it can only be at a certain point where there is the invitation in the spirit to go deeper. But, first, the carnal man has to reach this point of ripeness, which is about being mature enough to handle this depth of love. We cannot force our way into it because we are not agape love, obviously seeing why we cannot stir it up or make it happen.

(Sg. 2:8) We are in this deep intimacy listening for His voice in all matters and affairs. In the spirit, we are giving heed to His voice; we are being trained, and this growth enables us to listen for and heed His voice. Therefore, pictorially she is waiting; waiting is also in reference to inquiring of the Lord. Also noted is that in prayer, we may be surrounded by mountains and problems, yet He can overcome any mountain or problem, to reach us. No problem or situation is too big or a hindrance. *But all things are possible with God* (Matt. 19:26)

(Sg. 2: 9-10) He comes speedily to us. He is following His instinct: to come to our aid, saving His church; *like a gazelle or a young hart* (Sg. 2:9), He hastens to aid His church. Each of us resembles a church but also hastens to the life situation that we are in. Him standing behind the wall refers to us being in the old life, a wall between Him and us, before our salvation, but also regarding our prayer life. This is the point where He is purging us through the next step. He looks into our old life, old emotions, old willful ways of doing things, old habits, etc.; *he looks in through the windows, he glances through the lattice* Sg. 2:9) and calls us; come away with me; first in getting saved. After being saved in the purgation, we understand that there is a constant salvation in the purgation He is taking us through.

> *For, behold, the winter is past; the rain is over and gone. (Song of Solomon 2:11)*

Eveything that is frozen and locked up in our lives, everything that has not been able to touch the presence of Him in our lives, is being unlocked in deep intimate prayer with the Lord. Things we were unable to unlock, situations that have kept us in chains, past life hurts that have kept us in emotional prison are being released in His presence. Strongholds are broken in prayer because of His presence. It is the resurrection of our spiritual man into every circumstance. Our resurrection in our prayer life in Christ is that He is the only source of life there is.

> *The flowers appear on the earth; the time of the singing [of birds] has come, and the voice of the turtledove is heard in our land. (Song of Solomon 2:12)*

Sometimes when we start praying, we start from a really low point. We're caught up in the carnal emotions and thoughts, but as soon as He enters the door on the inside, we can suddenly see and hear, entering into the rest in God, and because of that, in the presence of Him, we are filled with hope; the situation is not so bad at all. In other words, our confidence in life and our circumstances are being restored through Him. The rejoicing in our hearts unfolds; *the time of singing [of birds] has come* (Sg. 2:12), and we automatically start to go into praise and worship. Out of that, we move in the spirit into an intimate love prayer; *the turtledove is heard in the land* (Sg. 1:11). Christ is displaying His love for us, and the result is us getting our hearts transformed into the heart of Christ. Out of this grows the love language in the spirit, which is expressed non-verbal; the Holy Spirit caresses our soul, restoring and loving on us as we love on Him.

## Chapter 16: Growing in the Intimate Relationship with God

*The fig tree puts forth and ripens her figs, and the vines are in blossom and give forth their fragrance. Arise, my love, my fair one, and come away. (Song of Solomon 2:13)*

Let's elaborate on the meaning of the fruits regarding prayer. Figs signify peace and prosperity; we have found peace in Christ and protection in Him. Figs don't mature at the same time, and it all depends on the climate. This is a picture of how we grow individually in Christ, and we need the right climate to live and grow. The fig tree can bear fruit but be uneatable; if we don't have the right climate to grow in, like the tree, we won't become mature ripe Christians. The fragrance of the vine flowers; the sacrifice in prayer often has to do with abstaining from giving in emotionally. It's a sacrifice for the carnal not to be able to do what it wants. This is the dying to self and signifies the ripe maturity in prayer. We start to mature spiritually when we stop giving in to the carnal cravings. When the time is right in prayer, *ripens her green figs* (Sg. 2:13), He calls us deeper into His presence in prayer. There is timing in prayer where we can go deeper. We wait, and He knows when to go deeper. It is an inner position of the heart that opens the door to go deeper. It is an inner alertness to wait on Him, and in the right timing, He is saying and moving in prayer: *arise, my love, my fair one, and come away* (Sg. 2:13). He is saying, I want to show you more about who I am and what I am really like. This rhythm is always ongoing in prayer; some layers of the carnal die, and then He can take us deeper into His presence.

*[So I went with him, and when we were climbing the rocky steps up the hillside, my beloved shepherd said to me] O my dove, [while you are here] in the seclusion of the clefts in the solid rock, in the sheltered and secret place of the cliff, let me see your face, let me hear your voice; for your voice is sweet, and your face is lovely. (Song of Solomon 2:14)*

We go along with Him in the Spirit; all done by Him; He is taking us deeper; He is guiding us into a small tiny area on the inner: *cleft* (Sg. 2:14), a small seclusive place where it is just Him and us. There is no room for anybody else. He surrounds us, and He is asking us to show ourselves; who we really are. He wants to see our face; in that, we realize we must willingly give up holding anything back from Him. He is here loving on us, showing us how beautiful we are to Him, and the hunger grows to be more and more with Him. Because He loves us, all we want is for this exchange of love to be constant in our lives. We come to realize that without Him, I am lost. I want to take out the part solid rock because that is very significant here. In Hebrew, it means retreat, strength, and place of concealment. That just very simply clarifies what is taking place in the prayer life that is hidden in the heart of Christ. When we willingly give up our life and say yes to the life offered in Christ, the return is the hidden safety place in the rock in Christ.

> *[My heart was touched and I fervently sang to him my desire] Take for us the foxes, the little foxes that spoil the vineyards [of our love], for our vineyard are in blossom. (Song of Solomon 2:15)*

The foxes represent our thinking in our prayer life; they resemble that our thinking in prayer can often distract us. She is asking Him to take hold of the foxes. If we transfer this into our prayer life, it would be like asking Jesus God to help us take hold of our thinking; to renew our minds with the thoughts in His mind for our lives. We need to learn to take hold of our thinking, taking our thoughts captive. We must understand that we can do that only through Christ. That is why she is asking Him to take hold of the foxes. However, it is still Him leading us to recognize the importance of renewing our minds; the Holy Spirit is pointing and convicting us in this area. When the Holy Spirit does that, the right timing is present; the anointing of renewing our mind is there. This is not just one occurrence, but this is something we will experience over and over in our purgation because there is a constant ongoing renewing in our sanctification.

Notice that she is first singing fervently to Him; that means we must understand the necessity that we minister to God by worshipping Him – first! All to empty ourselves focusing on one thing; the face of Christ, which makes everything else cease. If we cling to wrong thinking and allow it to come in through the door on the inner, it spoils the peace and the love in the relationship. It becomes a drawing away instead of drawing too. It is refined in the spiritual; sometimes, it takes very little to draw us away from the secret place. Therefore, we must understand that we must learn to become more and more ready to wait for longer and longer periods of time for Him in the secret place. The waiting is the security ground we stand and build upon. The secret key to waiting is where the inner transformation and purgation take place; like Christ's resurrection took place in the unseen tomb.

Likewise is our spiritual growth in Christ, which is in the waiting; nobody knows how - only God. God did the greatest transformation that ever took place, which was the raising of Jesus Christ from the dead. A mystery so marvelous and wondrous, one that holds such beauty because it made everything for all time whole and complete, and only God knows how. The allowance of God to perform in secret, and never reveal it openly, brings forth the fruit of displaying the finished work openly. Everything that He does must point back to the finished work of the Cross; it must glorify God. He does it in the same manner, transforming us within in secret, with us; it is the only way that God can use the vessel that we are. In this matter, God allows us to remember that it is Him doing the work within us, and we can never perform such wondrous work. Many people are untrained in the time it takes to wait; they want it fast and now, in the same manner and way as it is in the world. There is an increase in the rapid satisfaction of the flesh that the devil is displaying; we want a relationship with the Lord, to give satisfaction in the flesh, which will just as fast disappear as it entered into our lives; they won't last based on this ground. We must discern the difference between the ways of the devil and the ways of God; the devil is fast, and God is peace. That means we have to wait for the peace of God to rest upon us before we take action. The devil provides clever ideas without the heart in them. No wonder many people struggle to wait on anything, especially God.

We cannot tell the creator who created us how to make us; we must submit and wait for Him, and we cannot make a bargain with God, doing good to get a reward from Him.

We should be steadfast, learn to wait, and not be for sale at any price. We must never sell out on ourselves in fast decision-making because we must know that when we give in to that, we are making a bargain with the devil, the world, and the sinful nature. One can see that the waiting needs to unfold in many areas in our lives so that we will stay on the small path. Our prayer closet is the training ground for this to settle within. Learning to wait and yield in prayer is the key. This takes time to learn.

> *[She said distinctly] My beloved is mine and I am his! He pastures his flocks among the lilies. (Song of Solomon 2:16)*

When two belong together, there is a kind of unexplainable certainty. In that relationship, we know the other part won't leave us or withdraw even though we are not physically close. We know that the other part is always there. This certainty is the invitation not to always be in need of constant confirmation of the other party being in our lives. In other words, we don't need the other party to speak all the time or confirm that we belong together. In this place in our prayer life, He tends everything within us. Those areas that are untamed toward His presence, He tames through His love so that they will merge with Him: *flocks* (Sg. 2:16) so that our life becomes delightful, and we become able to rejoice and rest in peace: *lilies* (Sg. 2:16). He is lifting us up and is exalting our life in all areas, and it is an avoidable trade of the consequences of being in a relationship with Christ.

The Hebrew word for lilies has derived from *suws*, which means: rejoice, exult, glad, and delight, which is exactly what His presence will supply in us.

> *[Then, longingly addressing her absent shepherd, she cried] Until the day breaks and the shadows flee away, return hastily, O my beloved, and be like a gazelle or a young hart as you cover the mountains [which separate us]. (Song of Solomon 2:17)*

While He is working in our lives, clearing up areas: *mountains* (Sg. 2:17), we eagerly wait for Him; *Until the day breaks* (Sg. 2:17). There is only light in our lives when He is in our lives; *until the day breaks and the shadows flee away* (Sg. 2:17), and we can only go through difficult times in our life; *shadows flee away* (Sg. 2:17) when we are with Him. We wait patiently because, in this place, there is also the matter of faith to consider. He is looking to see if we are willing to wait for Him even though we can't see any change in our lives. Being in this place, we keep walking in the knowledge that He is working behind the scenes; however, the moment is not the time for us to see but to walk in faith. God is working on our inner in our prayer time; He is working on things that will separate us from Him if it is not dealt with. While we eagerly wait with a glad heart on Him and cannot wait to see Him, *cover the mountains* (Sg. 2:17). This is the ongoing purgation in prayer, Him working on the inner of our being, which we cannot understand or comprehend. For us, trust is growing in this place toward Him because when we come out of the prayer closet and into life, we know something is different, but we cannot explain how it happened. We know something is different because we act differently and do things we would never do or be. There is a deep inner change in our heart's position toward situations, people, and things in life. The trait of the fruits of the Holy Spirit comes to life within us, but we don't know exactly how. It is the mighty working of our Lord. All of this is also depicted as the mountains we need to overcome. The unseen life in the waiting. Simultaneously He is also working on the personal problems and the mountains we have in our lives. By this, we come to fathom that the Lord is always working on multiple levels at the same time.

(Sg. 3:1-5) *In the night I dreamed that I sought the one whom I love* (Sg. 3:1). These verses clearly show how lovesick we get for Christ. It is birthed in the night of darkness; *So I decided to go out into the city, into the streets and broad ways [which are so confusing to a country girl] and seek him whom my soul loves* (Sg. 3:2). A place of unrest and unease within; *I sought him, but I could not find him* (Sg. 3:2) also depicts areas and situations we cannot resolve ourselves. Being lovesick, as depicted here, has to do with the fact that there are some areas He has not yet touched upon spiritually, but we have tasted His touch in other areas, so we know how the change is experienced in our inner man. So, we long to live in that freedom of love. Only love and freedom are left when people are freed from hurts. In this state of change, the Lord uses everyday life circumstances to change us. The asking of watchmen and leaving them resembles other people who know of Him but do not know Him; it's a picture of how we cannot grow spiritually on other people's revelations or their walk with Jesus. *Scarcely had I passed by them when I found the one I love* (Sg. 3:4). We have to search and find ourselves. This is the only way we can truly find Him. Finding Him means that we come to understand Him and merge into the marriage with Him. *Until I had brought him to the house of my mother,* (Sg. 3:4) in this state we take Him into our hearts, *and into the chamber of her who had conceived me* (Sg. 3:4), into the innermost parts in such a way that we refuse to ever let go of Him again. Here the merging becomes undeniable.

In verse, *I adjure you* (Sg. 3:5), the Lord again reminds us that it is Him doing the inner work. The daughters of Jerusalem resemble unpurged emotions. *That you stir not up nor awaken love until it pleases* (Sg. 3:5), we cannot make the inner faculties surrender to God; the Holy Spirit does that.

There is an even deeper level of change in the carnal man. What is displayed in this state is the recognition of the sheer enmity of the flesh toward God, which took place at the fall of man. The death of the sinful nature is so horrifying for the carnal because, in this death, God shows us where we belong. It shows who it is compared to Christ Jesus God, and the horror of this is so dark and deep that it is always unbearable. The fear occurring in the carnal is a fear that moves the emotions, mind, and will into a state it never dreamed of existing. The Lord shows the environment where we belong. Darkness, which is a place so deep and vast, where we are left to be consumed by the hate of Satan. As if he is killing us over and over in this terrifying state. Abandoned by everything and everybody.

The Lord in His mercy shows us this very little at the time; this is done through a purgation in the process because we can't handle too much of this at the time, oftentimes only 3-4 seconds seeing oneself in this horrendous state of the carnal man. However, the change and effect of this in a person's life is just as extremely wondrous, a clear washing of purgation so unexplainable and marvelous; a deep and profound binding to the Lord Jesus is being formed and strengthened in these matters. Not many experience this layer of purgation, but on the contrary, stop because of the extreme unconformity in the flesh in reaching this point, and many think this cannot possibly be from God. Failing to comprehend how mysterious, unexpected, and different the Holy Spirit of God is because humanity has formed a God to their liking and not understanding who He truly is by heart. This is another way that God is teaching us discernment.

Yielded prayer implies the diligence of faith, arising on the inside to search for Him; we are moved by faith, hope, and love, and we will do everything we can to find Him. But, then, with desperation, we seek Him, and we are searching, *street and broad ways* (Sg. 3:2) for Jesus; the Holy Spirit initiates all of this; we cannot do this. This is how God initiated the way for us to search for Him. The love of Jesus Christ within us creates this kind of behavior, the natural behavior of the love of Christ moving within us. It is not quiet and polished; it is open desperation with fiery love displayed for all to see.

(Sg. 3:6-11) At a certain point in our walk with the Lord, the marriage takes place; the spiritual declaration of belonging together; it is a spiritual point of no return like the marriage depicts, the essence of the deep and profound love expressed. It is the declaration of where we proclaim to whom we belong. We are being taken away: *(the bridal car)* (Sg. 3:7), into full belonging in Him.

The salvation itself takes only an instant, just one word, yes, but it might take years before that yes comes to life; the process of growing in Christ. Then, out of that maturation, the inner yes to all circumstances, He is taking us through eventually takes us into the spiritual marriage.

(Sg. 3:9) Through the redeeming work of Christ and being raised, He *made himself a car or a palanquin* (Sg.3:9), the bridal car, so that He could come and deliver us to take us home into His eternal abode. Made out of all the royal elements, *pots of silver* (Sg. 3:10) depict the price He paid and is being upheld through the security that it can never be removed or shaken; it will stand forever. *The back of gold* (Sg. 3:10) sentence talks about how God's glory hovers above it, protecting it with His presence. The seat *of purple* (Sg.3:10) depicts us becoming kings in His royal palace, ruling and reigning with Christ. *The inside of it lovingly* (Sg. 3:10). Love and mercy are covering this carriage, which means the marriage between Christ and us is covered in the blood of Christ; it was bought and paid for.

All of this depicts the marriage supper of the Lamb, which is what will take place in the times of tribulation. Also, in prayer, we experience the Lamb's spiritual marriage supper in a miniature version.

In the spiritual marriage, there has to be a certain spiritual readiness that has to do with living a fully surrendered life to Him, and as one can see, this varies from person to person when and how this takes place. In both purgation and salvation, we see a need for a yes. The yes to salvation and the yes in the spiritual to grow in Him comes from the need to be saved in all areas of our life. We recognize that everything within us needs salvation and cleansing. Regarding living a surrendered life, we must understand that this implies dying to the carnal mind, emotion, and will. In this matter, we must comprehend that there are many different ways and depths of how to die, which will cause suffering. The Bible often speaks of this, and we see it throughout the Bible. The One who went through all suffering and enabled us to go through what each of us has to undergo was Jesus. Out of this, Jesus carries the crown of life in every area because of the redemption He fulfilled. The Bible teaches that we will receive different crowns on our path with Christ. For a king to receive a crown, he must conquer land before receiving it, and in war, it is always straining, difficult, painful, and hard. Likewise, we must fight spiritual battles. Only Jesus could undergo such indescribable pain and death. He was the only one who could drink the cup of salvation for mankind. Jesus had all the hordes of hell coming against Him, and He underwent the most excruciating physical death because of His sovereignty by being God to redeem the lost. God paid with the most expensive gift He had, His Son, to come and save us. Therefore, we must pay a price to walk with Christ. Otherwise, we cannot say we have sacrificed ourselves for God. As a result of the finished work of Jesus Christ, we come to terms that only through Him we can receive the spiritual and heavenly inheritance of eternal life. All of this we receive in the marriage with Christ. He so longs for us to be His bride forever.

We could not receive eternal life without Christ walking beforehand and taking all of our sins. We would be doomed forever if Jesus had not walked beforehand. It is very important to understand that we, in our carnal nature, are only worth being consumed by the wrath of God, and without Jesus, it would have been so. This is why salvation is the greatest gift given to mankind. In His mercy, we receive the inheritance without undergoing the equal pain of death as He went through. The fact is that it was a joy for Jesus to die for us. What a mystery.

This joy depicted in the love relationship is a deep joy and a deep pain when one is being separated from their spouse. God so longed to be with us, so He sent His only Son to come and redeem us. And because of that, we could enter into a marriage which is an allegory of belonging to each other.

> *Looking away [from all that will distract] to Jesus, Who is the Leader and the Source of our faith [giving the first incentive for our belief] and is also its Finisher [bringing to maturity and perfection]. He, for the joy [of obtaining the prize] that was set before Him, endured the cross, despising and ignoring the shame, and is now seated at the right hand of the throne of God. (Hebrew 12:2)*

Remembering these things, we understand the importance of prayer and that we are all united in the Body of Christ. Through an intimate prayer life in Christ, we can become the intercessory prayer people that we are called to be for each other. More than ever, we are in need of spiritual discernment, which comes through prayer; communion with Jesus.

## Chapter 4 is the love declaration.

(Sg. 4: 1-5) He is declaring His love for her, enabling her to fall in love with Him so that she becomes the one declaring her love for Him. This depicts the passion of our Lord for us. This is what Jesus did on the Cross; He declared out loud His passion for us, and we can now do the same because He did it first. We come to live for Him, and He gets to live through us, which is the most outspoken declaration of our love for Him. This is the ultimate way to show to whom we belong, just like He did with us, which is why we need to proclaim the Gospel. Preaching the Gospel is the love declaration we display. It is the same in marriage; when we tell to whom we belong, the confirmation through the yes. We declare out loud whom we love so that it is for all people and heavenly powers to know. That is why it is the strongest statement for us to proclaim. First, Jesus declared His love to us by saying and living it, and now we will do the same. God is not secretive with His love toward us, nor will we be. We would most desperately want to express this love; we cannot hold back on it. The Bible often talks about how God sees all affairs. When He looks upon a situation with favor, pleasing to Him, things come to life, and when He looks upon the situation with wrath, unpleasing to Him, things come to an end. When God sees it, He is knowledgeable of every circumstance and everything taking place. Seeing is knowing. It's the understanding that God knows all things. In chapter 4, the bridegroom praises the bride. In prayer, this means He sees and knows everything about us in the way we know. We stand spiritually naked before the Lord. We come to look so attractive to the Lord after going through the purgation and the cleansing, as we see described in these verses. The Lord sees the beauty in us that is arraying from our inner man. God looks upon the inner quality of the heart, morals, and integrity. The beauty He sees in her is here described in physical means. The description of the outer qualities depicts the inner qualities that He is looking out for to ripen within us.

**Going through the different aspects:**

*Eyes like doves* (Sg. 4:1), the innocent aspect transformed within us. *Your hair is like a flock of goats* (Sg. 4:1), which symbolizes our devotion to Christ. *Mount Gilead* (Sg. 4:1) is where the animal was kept in preparation to be sacrificed. This refers to how ready we are to be sacrificed for Christ constantly.

*Your lips are like a thread of scarlet and your mouth is lovely,* (Sg. 4:3), depicting how the blood of our Lord saves us. We are forever marked by this, for all to see: our lips.

*Your cheeks are halves of a pomegranate behind your veil (Sg. 4:3).* All the commandments are shown on our faces, which means they shine through our inner man. We are now filled with passion for our Lord. This occurs because we live and breathe what He has written on our hearts: His commandments. (Further details on pomegranates see appendix).

*Your neck is like the tower of David, built for an arsenal* (Sg. 4:4). We are no longer stiff-necked, doing our own thing. Now we have a beautiful neck like David, which was strong; we rightfully worship the Lord, just like David did. Through worship, an arsenal of power is available.

*A thousand bucklers* (Sg. 4:4), a numerous amount, refers to an infinite strength of protection; bucklers are only found in a righteous person. A righteous person is someone who lives by His truth. By that, His truth becomes our shield (Psalm 90:4)

*Your two breasts are like two fawns* (Sg. 4:5). Our faith and love for Him place us into the inner position of our hearts, which is like a child in His presence—being a child before Him is the safe place for us. This is how we come to reside in His tabernacle where we are feeding on His joy, lilies.

When the Lord has purged us in these affairs, we are now ready to lose ourselves entirely to Him. In prayer, this means that we give up any right to have and live our own lives. Now we only want to live for Him. We now realize in prayer that there is no life unless it is lived to and for Him. So, as she declares in the next verses, we declare that she is ready to choose Him under any circumstances. *I will get to the mountain of myrrh* (Sg. 4:6). She is now ready to undergo what He has in store for her. She is willing to lose sight of herself and, strangely enough, not knowing what she is saying yes to. It is the same with us in our walk with Christ Jesus. We don't know what kind of inner death He will take us through, but because the Holy Spirit is abiding within us, we can say yes without knowing how and in the knowledge that there will be difficult times. This applies in the purgation, as I have described earlier, which is the death of the carnal man and His love, which is frightening and strange for us in the flesh. *And to the hill of frankincense* (Sg. 4:6) We climb this inner mountain in prayer, yielding ourselves into the depth of His presence by waiting. Out of the inner death of the carnal man, only from here can the anointing flow. Many fail to know that the fear the carnal man experience on this journey with the Lord is inevitable. This is because the new life in Christ is so different from the life we live through the carnal man. When we are raised in this new life in Christ, we don't know how purgation and sanctification operate, how He will mold us, and what will happen. The nature of the Lord is so different from that of the carnal, and this is the reason for the fear in the carnal.

To put it in another way, how can something carnal comprehend something spiritual. In this matter, we must also consider the powers that operate in the heavenly sphere, surpassing everything man could ever understand or imagine.

There are two themes from this verse I would like to elaborate on in the context of what I have said. First, the Mountain of Myrrh is the mountain of Moriah, where the temple was built in which there was worship and burning of incense to the Lord. It was also the mountain where Abraham offered up Isaac, the residence of God, a place where one could seek and find Him and perform His precepts and commandments. Translated into prayer life; in His Holy temple, our heart, we seek Him, and we give away what is most important to us and ourselves. The meaning of the Hill of frankincense is as follows. Hill is derived from the Hebrew word *Geba*, which means cup or bowl, and frankincense is the sweet-smelling fragrance of the suffering of our Lord. These two combined show again the great Passion of our Lord on the Cross. We are drinking from the cup of suffering to turn it into a sweet-smelling fragrance before the Father. Jesus gave Himself away as we will give ourselves away.

Symbols are as follows:

- Frankincense: became a symbol of His priestly role
- Gold: resembles His kingship
- Myrrh: His death and embalming, and from that death, the anointing can flow. (Description is explained further below and in the appendix,).

There arises a yes on the inner to undergo suffering as our Lord experienced. Jesus didn't retreat from His calling, and by this, He enabled us not to depart, not of course in the same manner and depth, but we say yes to go all the way. As in a marriage vow, we say for better and for worse; it is the same here. We say yes to cling to Him during all circumstances, not to take us away from the difficult circumstances. Simultaneously, we also know and see the greatness of the reward. Because we are in the lineage with Christ Jesus, we are now His sons and daughters, which means we get to inherit everything that Jesus has. The temptation to lose sight of Him even in His glory or in the spiritual revelations or the favors from Him is close at hand. The more we receive, the more spiritually awake we need to be in order not to fall into the temptation of losing sight of Him, even though the blessings are from Him. This requires delicacy to His face. Only through the attention toward His face will solemnly keep our eyes on His love. We become spotless and: *no flaw in you!* (Sg 4:7) is a reference to the fact that we are cleansed by Him and made spotless/flawless. To outlive what He has provided, we need to spend time in yielded prayer. This also applies to the wording here regarding, we become beautiful. Only in Him, we become fair; we come to be righteous; *how beautiful you are* (Sg. 4:7). By this, we look so beautiful to Him, a reflected beauty of what He provided through the Cross. As a result, when we individually outlive our calling in Christ, the whole church can become whole in unity, and He returns to an unblemished church. The text here refers to us individually and as a whole. Therefore, we must understand by heart that what we do in the secret place has a direct consequence on the body of Christ; we are each of us responsible for our personal life in the knowledge that it has a direct influence on the body of Christ.

(Sg. 4:8) As in life, so it is in prayer; He comes and bids us come away with Him; first in life is through salvation, and then in our sanctification process where there is constant salvation, we need to participate in. This salvation purgation goes on while we are in prayer. He takes us away from our old lifestyle, *from the lions' dens, from the mountains of the leopards* (Sg 4:8) on the inner by renewing our thoughts. Attaining His thoughts, renewing our thoughts and emotions, transforming our inner man into His image. Spiritually we are being charged with the power and resources from His Spirit.

(Sg. 4:9-14) We become the lover He becomes intoxicated with; He repeats Himself like a passionate person lost in love; *ravished my heart* (Sg. 4:9). We must know that our relationship with Him is delicate and that He responds delicately. The Lord has a personality, which we can affect; to either come closer or withdraw. Here we see that by loving on Him by receiving the love He first poured out, we are now the ones to affect Him in a way to draw closer; *given me courage with one look from your eyes, with one jewel of your necklace* (Sg. 4:9). We come to look so beautiful to Him: *how much better is your love than wine!* (Sg. 4:10).

(Regarding verse 11, please see appendix). We see the seclusive private life, protected: *enclosed, and barred (Sg. 4:12)* by Him to which we now surrender fully in prayer. This inner fountain is sealed and locked up for Him; what He has given out to us, we now pour back by loving on Him.

We contain all the life-giving fruits and produce them in His presence; we come to look so beautiful because of that. We come to bear much fruit abiding in Him;

> *I am the Vine; you are the branches. Whoever lives in Me and I in him bears (abundant) fruit. However, apart from Me[cut off from vital union with Me], you can do nothing. (John 15:5)*

(Sg. 4:15-16) There is nothing trivial, repeated, and outdated about the love of Christ and the loving relationship; it is always fresh and new and is depicted as the fountain, the fresh well of water, digging deep into the well of Christ, His love. We long for His breath of life in us to blow in every area in our life; we come to truly understand in a profound way that only in Him and by Him we can produce any good fruit and by this do good. We fully understand to which extent the reverential fear of the Lord is abiding as our fellow companion in everything we do, that by ourselves we do only harm; bring death. We long for His abundance of life to spring forth, so much so that everything we want is for the carnal man to die as quickly as possible.

Only in Him is life; *Let my beloved come into His garden* (Sg.4:16), and we do it for Him in everything we do. Everything we long to worship is Him, and we fully understand that we do it for His name's sake and that everything, as a result, must glorify Him; *eat its choicest fruits* (Sg. 4:16).

## Chapter 16: Growing in the Intimate Relationship with God

*I have come into my garden, my sister, my [promised] bride; I have gathered my myrrh with my balsam and spice [from your sweet words, I have gathered the richest perfumes and spices]. I have eaten my honeycomb with my honey; I have drunk my wine with my milk. Eat, O friends [feast on, O revelers of the palace, you can never make my lover disloyal to me]! Drink, yes, drink abundantly of love, O precious one [for now I know you are mine, irrevocably mine! With his confident words still thrilling her heart, through the lattice she saw her shepherd turn away and disappear into the night]. (Song of Solomon 5:1)*

Summarizing this verse reveals the fundamental foundation that needs to be established as the foundation in our hearts; it thus sums up the complete work of Christ in our lives.

Through the purgation, we come to drink and eat the same food as Jesus; He sets the table and welcomes us in. Food is something we live off of and can give us a divine picture of spiritual growth. (See appendix). The spices balsam and myrrh were used to anoint people. They all contain an important spiritual meaning in our sanctified walk with Christ. (See verse 4:6). When we are saved and baptized, all spiritual life is available, but we must learn to wait and see the fruits these acts of obedience will yield through Christ. To grow spiritually, we need to receive stimulating spiritual discernment, depicted as food in the Scripture.

When the Word and our relationship with the Lord begin to deepen in earnest, the further we are on the path of walking with the Lord, testings, and trials can become more demanding, and an even deeper closeness with the Lord is required. We must remain a commitment to examine and investigate our lives in terms of which spiritual food we eat, making sure that what is in front of us is biblical food—referring to the description of food in the scripture. The world serves one kind of food, which we die from, while the Lord serves us food we can live off. Further details on the topic are below. Always investigating whether we are becoming more Christlike; do we become more unrecognizable to ourselves when setting the carnal man's death in motion so that we completely lose our taste for the old life?

This refers to what used to fill the carnal man, what he craved for. Things and matters that raise the carnal man to more splendidness in himself, which most often involve something enticing, and with appealing appetites for the carnal man, these are things that bring satisfaction. But, all of this must die. The step for us to consider is to know and contemplate; am I becoming more Christlike in all my affairs?

One could think that it would seem unnecessary to mention the studying and reading of the Word, but it is a trademark we should seek, always becoming hungrier for the Word because the devil would like to tell us how much we don't need the Word now that we have managed to come this far. Of course, in doing this, he is trying to lead us astray. In the beginning, even later in our walk, that carnal man also thinks that he doesn't need to read so much or that continuous study is just too straining. When we are first saved is not necessarily the beginning. That is implied, but addressing the beginning in the purgation, through this meaning that you might have thought that you have been walking with Christ for years, but then looking back at your life, you find no growth has taken place. This is what Paul is talking about when he addresses this issue:

> *Even though by this time you ought to be teaching others, you need someone to teach you the first principle of God's Word repeatedly. You have come to need milk, not solid food. (Hebrews 5:12)*

This growth applies to all the affairs and workings of Christ, through the purging and cleansing, alongside the mighty workings of the Holy Spirit: the signs, wonders, and miracles. However, we should not lose ourselves in these wonders lest we forget our first love, the face of Jesus. While this is a secondary point in this text, it is still an important one to mention. There is constant growth in all the faculties and affairs of the carnal man, a surrendering of them all to Christ. None must remain; they must all be purged in the cleansing fire of His love. Not one small little insignificant habit of the carnal man can remain; if something remains, then we can no longer say that all has been surrendered. This is the analogy of the Israelites needing to comply with every part of the Law, the 613 commandments, a duty they could not fulfill because they needed a redeemer. It is no different for us; in all our faculties and affairs, we need a redeemer to surrender to so we can be purged so that all can be surrendered to Him. In the analogy of the Israelites being unable to fulfill the commandments, they also did not have the right standing before the Lord, again as with us when we are not surrendering every part of our lives to the Lord. Because of this, we cannot enter into an intimate relationship with Him as He had intended.

In the Old Testament, it was forbidden to eat three-day-old food. This is an analogy that we are to read, study and spend time with the Lord every day, just like we are to eat fresh bread and drink fresh water every day. We cannot live off of old bread, yesterday's revelations. For the rest of our lives, we must grow. The seraphim surrounding the throne of God, day and night, never stopped saying:

> *An one cried to another and said, Holy, holy, holy is the Lord of hosts; the whole earth is full of His glory! Isaiah 6:3*

- based on constant new revelations of the Lord.

The Lord serves fresh bread and water every day; we should become thirstier and hungrier for this. Through the training we undergo in our purgation and transformation in Him, our spiritual discernment is honed; the purgation and the transformation are the keys to having discernment. Without being cleansed by the holy fire, we will stay unshaped and useless like the rough metal of a sword and will be no threat to the devil and therefore of no service to the Kingdom of God. Through the cleansing, we learn that the devil tries by all means at his disposal to serve us food that looks enticing, healthy, and tasty but is, in fact, poison to us that will surely bring death; mainly, of course, in trying to impact the emotions and our will. Spiritual death leads us away from Jesus, and we can no longer discern His voice. The devil works in a way in which the things we do seem like a good idea. This is the most common tactic he uses to lead us astray. This is also the most common mistake we read about in the Bible. The carefulness we always need to practice is based on the fact that the devil works bit by bit to move us slowly away without noticing that we are, thus explaining and proclaiming that the things we do are righteous. Without paying attention to where it comes from, asking and examining ourselves if it is biblical, this justification makes us fall away, even far away, for some never to notice, from the Lord. The greatest deceit he perpetrates is the slowly eroding yet convincing and persuasive voice speaking into our ears. In a supreme way, he is trying to convince people about the one trademark that always stands out: losing our fear of the Lord. Because he knows if this point is taken too lightly, the person will surely be lost. Now, if we hold on to caring about the fear of the Lord, we will reach great depths in our relationship with the Lord. Attacks from the devil enable us to grow and to be purged, thus, teaching us discernment. I must not fail to mention that later on, his onslaught becomes fearful and intimidating through physical and mental abuse, an onslaught that requires depth in our relationship with Christ. Otherwise, we would certainly die, either mentally or physically. However, most people don't reach this depth in their relationship with Christ and thus do not know this onslaught of the devil. However, these two are intertwined.

In this verse, the word my is repeated nine times, which is hugely important. One meaning in this context is the nine fruits of the Holy Spirit: the inner transformation received through Christ. First, He ate the food of the world and transformed it into spiritual food for the benefit of all mankind, and because of that, He made it possible for us to eat and gain life. The metaphor is the food; only through the food He serves can we attain life, and the life we can live comes from the fruits of the Holy Spirit. In the purgation, our taste for the world dies, and we gain the heavenly taste. Our world contains a different kind of food than the one Jesus has for us. Christ's invitation for us is to come and eat and drink what He is eating and drinking, but we can only eat and drink His food if we do it His way. This means that it is on His premises that we can eat, drink, be anointed, be perfumed, and so on. In other words, only His way works in receiving everything: anointing, being in communion with Christ. And first, when He knows by testing - by holding on to Him - that we belong to Him, we receive the anointing. Yet, this also is a sanctification process in going deeper into the well of what He offers. Remember Jesus was tempted in the desert, and His response was:

## Chapter 16: Growing in the Intimate Relationship with God

*But He replied, It has been written, Man shall not live and be upheld and sustained by bread alone, but by every word that comes forth from the mouth of God. (Matthew 4:4)*

He knew the Word and made it possible for us to resist because He did so first and finished this on the Cross. In this, He showed the way. Therefore, we have to know the Word today to resist. It is not God who is tempting us, but the tempter. That is the test and training.

The fruits of the Spirit are something that we can live off of, and we come to Him too. When abiding within Him, the fruits provide the nourishment we need: love, a calm and well-balanced mind, discipline, power, and self-control. And this is also the preparation for the afterlife:

*For God did not give us a spirit of timidity (of cowardice, of craven and cringing and fawning fear), but [He has given us a spirit] of power and of love and of calm and well-balanced mind and discipline and self-control. (2 Timothy 1:7)*

One definition of the meaning of power is this: power residing in a thing by virtue of its nature. It tells us very well when we are ripe to receive it: when our nature has turned its face toward Christ in virtue, and we solemnly look at Him. In the kingdom of God, the power of the miracles and the workings of God only moves through virtue/humility.

The fruit of the Holy Spirit is described in Galatians:

*But the fruit of the [[Holy] Spirit [the work which His presence within accomplishes] is love, joy (gladness), peace, patience (an even temper, forbearance), kindness, goodness (benevolence), faithfulness, Gentleness (meekness, humility), self-control (self-restraint, continence). Against such things there is no law [that can bring a charge]. (Galatians 5: 22-23)*

He is speaking of these fruits we come to eat from in the Spirit, voicing their trademark; we can live off them because they are the only real food. They are food for our spirit man, directly influencing our physical being. This we should keep watch over; growing in the virtue of the fruits of the

Holy Spirit enables us to come to live in a rightful place through a righteous living in all areas of our life.

The world's food is greed, money, carelessness, loneliness, isolation, and everything like it. Therefore, it shifts focus onto me. It is all about me. Whether we are down in life, where nothing goes well or right, or if we are up in life, everything is going our way. Both scenarios have one focus: me. None of them are of the Lord, and none of them is His plan for our life. We should neither be low nor blue, and we should neither be high nor mighty in ourselves as a continuous state of living.

The tempter comes with temptations and tries to steal our focus away from Christ. He either tries to throw us into the gutter with worry and confusion or tries to lift us on a pedestal, exclaiming our mightiness; this training is ongoing until the point is reached where the discerning spiritually is without doubt and clarity brought forth between the movement of the Lord and the enemy.

One could argue, is the way in which the Lord moves and abides obvious? However, in-depth in the purgation, the carnal man fails to recognize the Lord out of the loftiness of His nature and thus could very easily mistakenly take it to be of the devil. And regarding the devil, he comes disguised in sheep's clothing; he knows how to appeal to the carnal man and understands that the carnal is weak and has a soft spot for delightful affairs. In not being spiritually careful and attentive, the carnal man, in his weak nature, fails to recognize the devil. These soft spots, I must add, can only be truly fulfilled in the intimate relationship with Christ; to understand, the Lord has given man a soft spot for delightful matters and affairs, but it is meant for Him to fulfill them and not the ways of the world or the devil.

In these affairs, the purgation process is ongoing; thus, all matter brought before us has been placed to cleanse, educate and prepare us. Therefore, we have to go through the valley of the shadow of death, thus enabling us to know and recognize the tempter who tries to steal our emotions, thoughts, and so on, and in each incident abides a choice to stay focused on our relationship with Christ.

Another great importance of the number nine in this verse is the divine completeness, finality, and closure. Finality is something that has gone

## Chapter 16: Growing in the Intimate Relationship with God

through a process and then comes to a completion: but there has to be the process before one can have finality.

We never finish growing in Christ in our sanctification process; which is why He first tells the woman that she belongs to Him and then leaves her; and His leaving makes her more hungry for Him, which we will become growing in Him; more hungry:

> *O precious one [for now I know you are mine, irrevocably mine! With his confident words still thrilling her heart, through the lattice she saw her shepherd turn away and disappear into the night]. (Song of Solomon 5:1)*

There is, however, a place of perfection while being in an attainable body, which Christ longs for us to reach and abide in; all in all, to attain the unity of peace and love in Him; all in all, to grow further in these in the afterlife. This is depicted as a mini version of the Marriage Supper of the Lamb. Another remarkable thing about the number nine and the most essential work ever completed is that Christ died on the 9th hour of the day, or 3 p.m. Afterward, He rose and stripped the keys from Satan, enabling us to receive salvation. This was the completion of His life for us, allowing us to receive salvation and His heritage. The completion is depicted as the number nine working in time frequencies which we can see is not coincidental; in this way, the Lord shows Himself alongside in all of His affairs, moving in the foundation He has laid out before the beginning of time.

The night resembles something we don't understand; He comes in prayer when we are lying down. *I went to sleep* (Sg. 5:2), having the small death at hand; sleep symbolizes the dying to self and the old carnal nature. *Open to me, my sister, my love, my dove, my spotless one* (Sg. 5:2). He is coming to us in an unlikely, unexpected way and hour in prayer. He comes to us and seems to be needing us. We now have become the ones who can minister to Him pleasingly. We are now perfect, cleansed, and have the eyes of innocence; we have been washed clean in His blood, which means all carnality is gone.

Jesus sacrificed everything; *I am wet with [heavy] night dew; my head is covered with it.* (Sg. 5:2) He gave everything so that we could gain all things. Therefore, it can only be done through Him since He paid the price in full. He comes to bid her let Him in; He is in need of her. At this point, the Lord has molded us into His image in such a way that He can come to us. Not in any sense that we are perfect, only He is, but more in such a way like there is between two loved ones. While we are here on earth, we are the arms and legs of Jesus, and therefore He needs her.

(Sg. 5:3) Jesus comes unexpectedly when we are spiritually undressed; that's the place of a heart's full nakedness that He longs for in our hearts. We have taken off the old clothes, our self-righteousness. She is saying she is not ready; that's a picture of how the will is trying to take over by reason. We can't understand His ways: Him coming unpredicted, but we are to open the door at that moment when we think we are not ready. That's the picture of Him coming in the night. This is the place within a receptive heart that Jesus longs for. That is what makes the heart ready for Him; the off-guard position, just like a child, open and not caring about outer appearance; we have taken off our old clothes but solemnly care for the relationship. That very well depicts the nature of a child. He enters, and by His entrance into our hearts, we are moved; we forget ourselves.

(Sg. 5:4-5) He comes but does not stay; He touches that small place within; *My beloved put his hand by the hole of the door* (Sg. 5:4), yet not entering fully, but seemingly to us we expect Him that He will enter now, only to realize Him leaving again, which leaves us in a state of longing even more for Him. That serves the whole purpose of Him doing so. The sweet loveliness of His presence leaves us in agony when suddenly He is gone. It is just for a moment because we are not spiritually purged enough or cleansed enough, so He creates a situation in which He leaves us to make us long even more through carnal death. He leaves the anointing oil: *myrrh* (Sg. 5:5). Myrrh resembles the death of Jesus on the Cross. Likewise, we will go through death in the carnal purgation, and in that death, anointing oil can flow on the handles on the bolt just a little bit to create a deeper longing within. This is a picture of the spiritual growth He takes us

## Chapter 16: Growing in the Intimate Relationship with God

through. It is always a little bit by bit; it seems like that. Our lives start to move in the right direction because of the overflowing of His love for us, in the sense that only in Him is there life. We begin to experience the favor from Him. By this precept of the Lord, we must understand that whatever He sheds His light on will be. His light is who He is and where He is, there is light; also meaning what does not bring life will be removed; to understand that only that which is life in and through Him will stand. Therefore, we experience the passing of the old in every area of our lives; meaning that which in the eyes of our Lord is dead; having no life, will cease to be. Little by little, it is all the flesh can handle of His love, later more and more. Yet even when it is more, it still seems and is little because we tend to get hungry for His love. Later we can eat more bread and contain more of His love, but it still seems like a small portion; this is the purgation. This continues throughout our life because there is always more to deepen in His presence. So, the previous experience we had, in that moment of anointing, will always be the next step we stand on or move from to move higher and deeper in prayer.

(Sg. 5:6) He has now turned away, and we experience the sheer pain when He is not nearby. In this relation, we constantly grow into wanting more of Him in closeness; so, when He comes closer to us, it would seem to our heart that He is even further away because we go deeper and deeper into His heart. Therefore, we always want more of this intimate relationship in our hearts to merge; yet it merely keeps getting deeper and deeper.

*They stuck me, they wounded me* (Sg. 5:7). We go searching for our love; we are bruised and wounded; we are being stripped of our belongings in search for Him. We are being persecuted physically because, by that, we are purged spiritually.

(Sg. 5:8-9) People don't understand us, and they don't understand the depth of intimate prayer relationship; because most people, not even the ones who should, don't know this truth: *daughters of Jerusalem* (Sg. 5:8). Our love for Him overflows and compels us to go and preach the Gospel, telling them about this love; we are lovesick, and all we have left in life is Jesus. In this place, we understand that life only exists through Jesus. We are being stripped bare to the core of our being; we die to the old lives and wants, and we preach with all of our hearts because we understand the meaning of life: to walk, live and be with Jesus.

(Sg. 5:10) We come to understand by heart that Jesus is righteousness; He is life; He contains all emotional traits. Above all others, He is the King of Kings.

(Sg. 5:11) We come to understand that His head is as pure as the finest gold. In understanding that Jesus is the head of the church, we realize He is the most precious one in the church; without Jesus first in all things, no church exists. That is why His head becomes the most precious one for us; we see life not being led and sought first in Christ in all things, then it is not life, then it is living stones. His locks, curls: young life, meaning the renewed life in Christ is the expression of life moved out of His head, the church. Bushy; is the trail that shapes us in prayer and into the church. By the trails, He guides us to the small path found in prayer. It is small because we need to pay close attention and listen. Black is the unseen ways of the Lord and in it is the humiliation we undergo in search of Him.

(Sg. 5:12) The Bible refers to the eyes as the doors to the soul. They reflect the inner innocence of Jesus seen in His eyes. His are shimmering dazzling beside the waters; they reflect the deep veil of His love. He looks so attractive to our heart; He speaks to our heart in a secret language that we don't understand but is being moved in our heart, compelled by His love; His love takes over.

He is so innocent, worthy, pure, and clear: *milk* (Sg. 5:12) that everything comes together: *fitly* (Sg. 5:12).

(Sg. 5:13) The word cheek contains a Hebrew meaning *soft*; we become soft; we surrender in His presence; we die in the carnal man in His presence. It is the picture of a person being so in love that one is being compelled by love, so much so that one doesn't care any longer if one loses one's own will; that's the death of the carnal man. We are in prayer here, being killed by His love. His love takes out the enmity of the carnal toward God. It is so sweet; His love is a well-scented fragrance to us; we are consumed by it. All the sweet-scented smells, tastes, and looks enable us to lose ourselves in His arms completely; the attention of His loveliness draws us naturally away from ourselves. From His lips, when He speaks, comes forth the truth with such an anointing, sweetness, and joy that it makes us able to stand. The Word is the only thing that will remain throughout all time. Everything else will disappear, and only the Word will live; so, when Jesus speaks to us, we are being fed with what is life. Our inner man is strengthened every time. Out of this is brought forth an overwhelming joy which is expressed like when David brought in the Ark; dancing, praising the Lord, losing oneself to Him over and over. Bloodred: life; He gave up His; the blood was shed; equally gained ours; the precious blood of Jesus; the purification of the blood. In prayer, we come in a revelatory way to understand by heart the Cross; in ways and in-depth that change us radically, all in all, because the blood is alive today.

(Sg. 5:14) He holds all power: rods, steadfast and unchanging. His ways are pure: gold. His nails are covered with topaz. It derives from the Greek word *topazios,* which means to seek; He is searching us out to set things in order so that our lives may align with the plan He has for us. He points the way to shed light on our situation so we may follow Him. His body being of bright ivory refers to the purity of Christ. Overlaid with sapphires, looking at the Hebrew word, we see that it derives from: to score with a mark, to inscribe, to enumerate, recount, to celebrate, to commune. These marks are the trademarks of Christ upon our lives when we walk with Him. These are the steps of being intimate with someone. In this incident, we are becoming intimate with Christ in a dependent love way in which we only see His beauty.

(Sg. 5:15) He is our strength; in Him, we stand; *His legs are strong and steady pillars of marble* (Sg. 5:15) Steadfast, unmovable; we can count on Him; He is unchangeable and faithful. His foundation is pure: gold. His appearance is like Lebanon: excellent, stately, pure as white. The Hebrew *laban* means *white*: stately, like a mountain, exulted high, lifted up, unmovable; a purity as solid as a mountain. Nothing can defile it; it has been made clean by the blood of Christ on the Cross. This washing of purity within comes first in our saying yes to Christ Jesus as our Lord and Savior. Out of this, yes, there is a continuous depth of the well of love being poured out. The continuation of this outpouring that springs forth from the inner well of Christ is referred to as the mountain. The giants that are working against us, the mountains, will bow down to the greatest mountain: Jesus Christ. There are biblical mountains or giants, which are spiritual powers that are working against us that only Jesus can eliminate. Therefore, there is a reference to God dwelling in Mount Zion (Heb. 12:22), Him being the highest authority, therefore above them all. Mount Carmel is a spiritual picture of defeating the spiritual powers (1 Kgs. 18:36-39). Everything He is and does is worthy: *majestic as the cedars* (Sg. 5:15). He thereby makes our lives worthy to Him and gives us worthy lives to live. It also refers to all the unworthy things in our lives when we meet Him. He will put into order and straighten out our lives in a worthy manner. We get to receive an excellent stately, and worthy life. In this sense, it is not referred to the physical riches of life, even though they will follow automatically when we follow His footsteps, but an inner richness and abundance in Him. With His appearance, stately and excellent, we come to stand strong. Cedar is the hardest tree and has a very long duration. It was one of the most expensive sorts one could buy in ancient times, hence a synonym for the wealth of life we receive in Christ. It is full of resin, which preserves it from rot and worms, referred to as something that won't decay but last. We come to understand it is a picture of His Glory.

(Sg. 5:16) When we describe Him, we preach the Word, and we also come to understand more about His loveliness in every way. When He speaks to us, life is being poured into us. This revelation we come to understand by heart in every way. All of our being has been purged so that when we see that Jesus is the living bread of life, we come live on His bread alone. We are spiritually fed by every word He speaks to us; at this point, we realize that our soul is being fed from the Word of God. We understand here the depth of the nourishment that we receive from Him, and because of Christ through the Holy Spirit, we come to understand the connection in the Trinity. He becomes our everything; *this is my beloved, and this is my friend* (Sg. 5:16). When we come to see and understand by heart all the trademarks of Christ; we are being transformed into them, and thereby we recognize who He is in us; we come to live them ourselves.

(Sg. 6:1) When we talk about Him, the Holy Spirit stirs people up in their hearts; people who are the lost bride: [*Again the ladies*] (Sg. 6:1). The Word of God is alive, and that truth cuts them in their hearts. The conviction of the truth brings forth the life of Christ within; therefore, they ask where we find Him. When we speak the Word of God, His love brings forth the conviction through the Word, thus cutting out that which is not the truth. In (Acts 2:37) we read that people were cut to the heart; the old life was cut away; their hearts were cut open to the truth of life that Peter spoke of, and because of that, the lie falls away because the words Peter spoke brought forth conviction and revelation. This is the occurrence of speaking the Word of God, and it brings life.

> *[She replied] My beloved has gone down to his garden, to the beds of spices, to feed in the gardens, and to gather lilies. (Song of Solomon 6:2)*

(Sg. 6:2) Jesus came down on earth, fulfilling the plan for the body of Christ, the church, which is the garden. The Father is the keeper of the garden, and Jesus is the vine from where the branches grow: us (John 15). Here we also see a mystery in the Trinity being revealed; He is the Keeper and the Gardener. He is our food in every way; He is our life. This also applies to our hearts; He needs to reside and abide in our hearts; hence He is the only one who can keep our hearts, the analogy of Him keeping the garden.

(Sg. 6:3) She describes what it is like to be His garden and know Him well in this intimate relationship. She speaks in a tone that makes one would desire it as well. All in all, the heart is constantly stirred up and deepened into His love. She describes herself as a garden, resembling a church. He feeds among the lilies; in the joyous and peaceful moment, He is feeding us; only in His peace and joy are we being fed.

(Sg. 6: 4-8) Describes His longing for us; we are now worthy of Him describing us in this manner. Now we reflect on the beauty of Him because the nature of the carnal is of no more. This is the picture of a spiritual merging. We hear the love language He is speaking to her; in prayer, we are close to the Lord, and our heart's desires have become one with His. Therefore, we appear so beautiful to Him. The way He is pursuing us is found in the description of her. *Your teeth are like a flock of ewes* (Sg. 6:6). We are now spiritually ripe to listen like a full-grown women. A woman has to do with being able to care for the right affairs in life. Not regarded as a gender point. So now we can chew rightfully; *all are in pairs* (Sg. 6:6) to receive the full measure from the Word. See verses 4:1, 5:11, and the appendix for further details.

(Sg. 6:9) In this constant purgation of submission toward Him, we come to stand out, and we are noticed for all to see. His love is displaying us, and His love within us He is using to display His glory. We are abiding in His love. She is constantly seeking His love; we are in this place continually seeking Him.

(Sg. 6:10) It becomes increasingly evident that we are being transformed into His image for all to see and recognize. The sanctification has touched us in every way; the fruit of the Holy Spirit is evident.

(Sg. 6:11-12) It is the centrality of Song of Solomon because it describes what Jesus did on the Cross.

> *[The Shulamite replied] I went down into the nut orchard [one day] to look at the green plants of the valley, to see whether the grapevine had budded and the pomegranates were in flower. Before I was aware [of what was happening], my desire [to roam about] had brought me into the area of the princes of my people [the king's retinue]. (Song of Solomon 6:11-12)*

(Sg. 6:11) To come up, one must come down. There is a timing in prayer where we come down and deep; we cannot decide or produce this timing; only the Lord knows of this timing. Therefore, the text says one day, she went down/descended. Through this waiting and timing in prayer, we are searching out; *to look at the green plants* (Sg. 6:11). We have to search for the ripeness of the timing in prayer. Hence until the situation is ripe, we wait. That is the actual searching. We look, being spiritually awake in prayer for us to be able to see and go deeper; *whether the grapevine had budded and the pomegranates were in flower* (Sg. 6:11). When we see plants budding, we then, for a fact, know that the new is coming into our life. The life Christ has provided for us is now showing off, bearing fruit. It is now very visible that the old life is dead. For a seed to be sewn into the dirt, it must die; it must be broken open for the new life to spring forth. Out of the seed placed in the dirt, we know that new life can grow and bear fruit.

There are three stories of breaking open our inner alabaster jar in the dying to self and recognizing in our heart our nature and the nature of Jesus Christ. First, the old must die for more crops to be produced like our Lord. So He died, and out of that, the Father received many sons and daughters (Matt. 26: 7-13, Mrk. 14: 3-9 and Luk. 7:37-38).

## Grapevine

The crushing of the grapevines and the vine being spilled is a picture of the sins the Lord took on the Cross in giving up His life for ours. Every drop of His precious blood was given up for us.

This He gave up so that it enabled us to produce grapes, fruit, anew. The Bible says that we shall do greater things than Jesus, and since He is now the One interceding for us before the Father, only, therefore, we can do greater. We can never be greater than Jesus because no one could do what He did; only He could redeem us and place salvation as an opportunity before us. These greater things are being displayed here as the grapevines are flowering. We become the right arm or the left foot of Christ, the body of Christ; by this, we shall do greater things. We need to be seeking and asking Him first because it is Him that is interceding before the Father, thus, meaning and making it very clear that all affairs are done through the workings of Christ. We are merely but a lump of clay, asking in the name of Jesus.

*I assure you, most solemnly I tell you, if anyone steadfastly believes in Me, he will himself be able to do the things that I do; and he will do even greater things than these, because I go to the Father. And I will do [I Myself will grant] whatever you ask in My Name [as presenting all I AM], so that the Father may be glorified and extolled in (through) the Son. [Yes] I will grant [I Myself will do for you] whatever you shall ask in My Name [as presenting all I Am]. (John 14:12-14)*

This fine and subtle place in prayer entering through the door of the heart on the inner is depicted in describing the nuts orchard. They require favorable conditions to grow, particularly in the mountains in Palestine and around the lake of Gennesaret/Sea of Galilee. A grove of such trees provides the most delightful shade; we are protected under the Lord's mighty wings and produce fruit: the walnut under the right conditions. In this matter, we can see Christ's reproduction; hence He is here represented as the walnut tree. *Egoza*, which means nut, has the numerical equivalent of the letter in *het*, which is the Hebrew word for sin. So, our sin is taken, and by that, we receive the fertility of life, meaning we are transformed into His image. This fertility of love we reproduce by showing love toward others; the centrality of the message of the Gospel of Christ Jesus for our lives. The Lord has a garden for us to grow in, a protected area where there is a hedge of His glory of life and love around us, and because of that, we have nothing to fear. Adam and Eve were also placed in a garden, hedged in, a place where they could continue to live the life God had created them to be. After the Cross, we now have the same opportunity because of Christ Jesus. This is what we gain when seeking Him; in the thickness of His glory, we stand naked as Adam and Eve; nothing to fear. Everything within us is exposed freely and joyfully before Him; we don't want to hide anything from Him because we know in hiding, there is separation from our loved One. His glory now becomes our raiment, as it was with Adam and Eve before the fall. Only in His garden, His presence, and thereby glory, do we get to overcome our trials, depicted as yellow: sin. And with His Word: blue, truth enables us to become resurrected: green: salvation, new creation, in every area of our life.

All things abiding in the garden represent a spiritual meaning that comes to pass through the breaking of sinful bonds Jesus fulfilled on the Cross.

The meaning of the pomegranates in (Sg. 6:12) (See appendix). (Sg. 6:12) She loses herself in His love; *before I was aware, [of what was happening], my desire* (Sg. 6:12). We lose ourselves, and prayer requires this point of forgetfulness to oneself, which the Holy Spirit brings forth. The sweet caress of the Holy Spirit; the sweet caress of a mother. The anointing oil of the Holy Spirit is the sweet caress we thirst for because it is Christ's love pouring out of and through us. We are then lifted up; she is carried away in a chariot; our soul is lifted up in prayer: rapture.

(Sg. 6:13) The attractiveness of His love within us makes us attractive to people who don't know Him. This is how we recognize Him, and we find how absolutely nothing we are without Him, and we don't want people to recognize us because we realize this is not something we can do or be. We owe it all to Him who gave Himself away on the Cross, so we constantly give ourselves away for Him. Humbleness is the forthcoming trait that shines; *What is there for you to see in a [poor little] Shulammite?* (Sg. 6:13).

(Sg. 7:1-6) The purgation is evident; His virtue starts to move through us in a noticeable way. We come to have influence through outer appearance, which symbolizes the inner spiritual authority or influence. Satan now knows our voice in the spiritual realm, and we understand by heart the meaning and the responsibility of carrying His name. The riches of God also bestow upon our lives; the King sees our attractiveness. *Your head crowns you like Mount Carmel* (Sg. 7:5). Our thought is full of life and wisdom. Virtue emanates from our inner man, from our heart; we have the mind, and heart, of Christ. However, still walking out of our sanctification. Christlike, but never as Christ; that we can never be. Jesus took the crown of thorns and replaced it with the crown of life for us. Most of the descriptions in these verses have already been elaborated on previously.

(Sg. 7:7-9) There is a recognition from the Lord; we now look so lovely to Him because we reflect the truth. When the Father looks at us, He no longer sees us but sees Jesus. This took place, first on the Cross and afterward in being saved. Yet there is a purgation to undergo for that which is the maturity of Christ within us to be poured out.

(Sg. 7:10) We proclaim to whom we belong; we proclaim this everywhere and to all; preaching the Gospel of Christ; [*She proudly said*] (Sg. 7:10), which is love; which is Jesus; we are no longer ours. Nothing can take us out of the hand of God's love for us. This revelation we now openly display and know by heart; we belong to Jesus.

(Sg. 7:11-13) We now desire to go out and give ourselves away to Him; we openly talk about this love. We have now died to ourselves. In that, we become an empty vessel He can use; we no longer exist for ourselves. We come to exist for Him; we become the bondservant of the love of Christ Jesus.

(Sg. 8:1) Brother: same blood; a picture of the intimate closeness. Also, a picture of the lineage with which we are now in the family; to whom we belong; an unbreakable bond. And by this, it also means a deep-rooted connection, which is indestructible regarding a family member, someone you love the most. Because of this connection, we are now continuously open toward Christ. As a family, we wish to share and care for each other. When we are babes, we are nurtured through our mother's breast. This reflects the same intimate closeness we come to live in toward Christ and the same nourishment we live in through our prayer life. The nourishment of love from Him to us we now live on and from. If we find Him distant in prayer, the intimate closeness is not as deep, and we would then kiss Him and worship Him and love on Him. Loving on Him is brought forth from the knowledge of having the reverential fear of the Lord. In ancient times a kiss was given to show respect, subjection, and affection. Through the worship and kiss, we return to the inner heart well of Christ.

> [*Then musingly, she added*] *Oh, that his left hand were under my head and that his right hand embraced me! (Song of Solomon 8:3)*

(Sg. 8:3) Inner deep surrender is taken place, and He is upholding us in a lover's embrace. We are again lost in His arms of life. His strong and mighty arm is fighting our every battle so that we may enter into the rest of

Christ Jesus; Jesus is our Sabbath. In this secret place, we don't care about time; we don't care about anything else than having Him holding our head in the closeness of Him embracing us. We give ourselves in time to Him because we lose the sense of time; we are so in love with Him. All we want is to give ourselves to Him. We want to be overtaken by this consuming love. And we experience Him surrounding us with His love; in His protecting arms in the spiritual.

The Hebrew meaning of the word bosom is: cherish, care, base, hold firmly, and is derived from the root wording in Hebrew, which means to love.

(Sg. 8:4) Again, only He knows the timing in our life and prayer, and only He knows the timing in coming through the narrow gate to enter into His heart. Therefore, she is adjuring them; in prayer, we must be cautious of falling asleep in the spiritual by thinking that we know the Lord, in a sense that we don't come fresh in the spirit before Him; so, we have adjured ourselves, being awake. There is a warning in this, and many think they are in this loving, intimate relationship with Christ when it has moved them into imaginary thinking and emotional hype where they think they are in this loving relationship. This happens when we push ourselves instead of letting the inner flower of the heart open, for which only He knows when the right time. A fake loving relationship in which they think they are close, and the result is pride. The problem with pride is that it thinks it knows. The result is that it thinks it knows the Lord when the pride unknowingly moves the person further and further away from the Lord.

(Sg. 8:5) We come from wilderness into life; we are leaning on Him; we are awakened, raised up, in Him; we spiritually come to life in Him; we understand by heart what it means to see and hear. We come to understand we cannot produce anything; no anointing, no life, and because of that, we lean on Him. He is our Rock of life, in prayer as well. We cannot produce peace or purgation, only in Him when we close our eyes and lean on Him. It is a secret transformation because we will never fully understand how it happens. When Jesus was raised in the tomb, nobody knew or saw but God. We are under His protection, and there is delight and fruit in that place. She compares Him to an apple tree; *I delighted to sit* (Sg. 2:3). We rest in Him, and *His fruit was sweet to my taste* (Sg. 2:3). Only He brings the sweetness of life into our life.

Being raised or awakened is the church awakened; hence every one of us is the church.

(Sg. 8:6-7) It is the ultimate picture of our love for Him, the ultimate knowledge of not wanting to lose the intimate relationship with Him, terrified of being led off. We especially become very aware of our carnal nature, which is the ultimate enemy, because we know we cannot in any way count on it. A zeal is something that is locked into each other forever, in this matter; a love pact with Jesus Christ. Love is as strong as death; Jesus died for us; His passion of love until death for us. The same love affair occurs within us in giving ourselves away to die for Him. Nothing of the world can draw us away from Him; we'll despise it in the sense that nothing can compare to the inner completeness of love. Nothing from the world can bring forth such a depth of love and completeness as with Him. We have received this in a revelatory way so that we can resist the temptation of things with which Satan, the carnal, and the world try to deceive us. We have become spiritually awakened to recognize from whence things or situations derive. We can here sense the subtleness of the nature in life. The scales have fallen from our eyes, and we can see. Likewise, the scales have fallen from our ears so that now we can hear.

(Sg. 8:8) No breasts; not mature spiritually in Christ, also the newborn Christians for whom we need to care and how we do that as a church. Little sister; those younger in Christ, is in relation to prayer and it's attributes and emotions resembling that which are not fully developed in the death of them, not having been purged unto death in them, to which we need to pay attention by protecting these areas until we are spiritually grown.

(Sg. 8: 9-10) Here we, that is her telling her stepbrothers, come to understand by heart the difference between being a mature and an immature Christian. When we can define that, we are mature; hence we know the difference. She is telling them what they thought of her if she would not be ready for marriage, the unity with Jesus. She tells them that integrity is one of the most prominent signs of spiritual growth: *if she is a wall [discreet and womanly]* (Sg. 8:9). It also shows emotional restraint, one of the surest signs of spiritual maturity, because we know we cannot restrain emotions. When this is purged within us so that only integrity is left pure inside, we are released from that which holds or restrains us because we come to understand spiritually that we have been bought with a price: silver; the Israelites paid ransom or redemption money as a poll tax to make the 100 silver sockets in the tent of the tabernacle (Exo. 30:12-16, 38:25-28). Resembling the price, we were bought through Jesus Christ on the Cross. Silver also stands for truth; we come to comprehend the truth in His love and through the Word.

The dowry is what we receive through our holding on to the integrity through what the relationship with Jesus Christ molds us into. We now become worthy of having them build a turret; it is part of a larger tower, typically of a castle, here resembling us in being part of the church, the body of Christ, and the need for the church. We become the foundation that the Lord has molded us into, and upon that, He can build a place where we can now see and hear spiritually, not only for ourselves but for the church as well. We can now be used as a wall of protection for others. The body of Christ becomes our family by heart. Our hearts have been intertwined with God and purged into an overflowing passion and compelling love for people through that with other Christians because we now carry the heart of Jesus Christ. Through this molding, we enter into His rest as well: *Then was I in [the king's] eyes as one [to be respected and to be allowed] to find peace* (Sg. 8:10).

(Sg. 8:11) *Ball-hamon*: possessor of abundance; the Lord has the place of an abundance in all areas of our lives, and He is the possessor of the multitude. In His garden, in His church, we are the entrusted ones to be the keepers of the garden. Here we come to grasp the gifts He has laid within each one of us, and thereby we come to fathom the importance of the body of Christ. Hence all gifts are equally important. In combining the one thousand pieces and silver, which symbolizes the redemption money Jesus paid for us, the thousand means fullness of quantity; we see the ultimate freedom the Lord provides for us in being under His covenant and grace.

We also come to fathom that what we give, pay; *everyone was to bring him a thousand pieces of silver for its fruit* (Sg. 8:11) we receive again; therefore, we never really paid it. He did. We come to fathom more and more when working in His garden. Jesus spoke of parables concerning working in His garden and how we use our talents. (Matt 25:14-30 20:1-16) The landowner and the workers (Matt. 21: 33-46). We must notice the warnings in these parables; we can very easily come to think that it is ours; the flesh is weak. In this matter, we must pay close attention to the response of our flesh when things go well.

(Sg. 8:12-13) We see how she has welcomed the gift of grace by living in the garden; we now recognize what Jesus has provided for us; we fathom the importance of the workings of the Cross. We can only really rest in the garden when we understand by heart that He gave it for us to rest there. Instead, we give all God's gifts away rather than lose Him, which is why we can now carry the grace of the virtues. That is the spiritual attitude and understanding we need to rest in Him, and we can read that she knows it's not hers, for she easily and willingly wants to give it back to Him and even the tenants. This is how we come to behave; willingly, we would want to give away to other fellow men what He has provided for us in the garden. The two hundred is two times a hundred, which resembles the double honor or portion He provided for us. Through us, the Lord receives His fruit in return, a hundred-fold (Matt. 13:8-9). The spiritual authority He provides in our lives we now gladly give away. This is walking in the narrow way of growing in intimacy in Him; this is his pattern we are copying from Him. He gave Himself away, stripped Himself of all power, came low, and received even more sovereignty, rule, and supremacy. This is the revelation we receive in Him; it is freely given, and the rest, Sabbath, is provided from Jesus Christ; *O you who dwell in the gardens* (Sg. 8:13). We read that she willingly gives it all up if only she could be with Him. We behave in the same manner; nothing has a hold on us any longer, not even the things provided to us by Jesus, because we know it all belongs to Him.

We have now found our garden within Christ, our sanctuary place in Him. *Your companions have been listening to your voice* (Sg. 8:13). There is a voicing up in our prayers out of this love because of the place of abiding within His garden; our home, we cannot help ourselves sing praises to His name. So much so that He longs to hear it. In this place in prayer, we are ministering to Him.

Taken into consideration that it is not only one person that is lifting up their voices in prayer. It is the whole body of Christ. In this, there arises a longing to hear the voice of the others, fellow Christians, because we are the body of Christ. We so long to hear everything God is speaking through everyone. This creates the fellowship and strong unity in the church; only by this strong unity in seeking Him will the church prevail, recognizing and paying close attention to when the Lord is moving upon the gifting in the church. The five-fold ministry comes into complete alignment (Eph. 4:11-13), and by this, the church will stand its ground. There are many others gifts, but these are the ones that hold a foundation in the church. There has to be recognition of each other in church. This we constantly long for, to be, and live in. We also need to pay close attention to this in church; the church loses its unity when people only look out for themselves. A united church is the mightiest weapon against the adversary, which is exactly why the enemy has put this "individual self-preservation" in church; he knows it will be the church's downfall if it succeeds.

(Sg. 8:14) We see how the anointing oil, His liquid love, is now overflowing in our lives, not only on us but also in all areas of life. A short throwback on some previous verses before moving on:

In verse (Sg. 2:17), we see it started as a fear of losing Him, out of love, and then arises, fear of division. We have recognized that we cannot make it or live without Him; we long to be with Him; we eagerly await Him. We are spiritually untrained because we still look at the things or situations; here, depicted as the shadow and that the night is long without Him.

We also come into the depth of having the reverential fear of the Lord because we by now have come to experience His might and power in our lives, Him saving us over and over in various situations. This also leads us into a depth of the scarcity of losing Him.

Then in verse (Sg. 3:6), we see some spiritual growth take place; we know that situations and things will change in our lives. She is waiting for the shadows to leave and for the day to break in her mind. She now knows she must go to the mountain of myrrh and the hill of frankincense. At this stage in our purgation, we understand that we must wait for the oil to overflow in our lives and for His love to take over. We are getting to awaken the spiritual sensory system and move by it in prayer, letting the Holy Spirit take over. We now understand by heart; that it is all work done by the Holy Spirit.

Here in turning to (Sg. 8:14), we see the overflowing of the liquid love overrunning our lives, a security of Him not leaving us. We have now come to the point of naturally letting the Holy Spirit take over; *upon the mountains of spices!* (Sg. 8:14) as a deeper and deeper overflow. This growth of depth comes through our time with Him. We can't wait to grow deeper and deeper into this intimate relationship; *Make haste, my beloved, and come quickly, like a gazelle or a young hart* (Sg. 8:14). We are merged into His love and presence; this is all we want and long for. The Holy Spirit makes us long and creates this longing for Him.

Waiting for Him to come over the mountains is mentioned many times. We are standing in one place in prayer, oftentimes in no or very little movement. This corresponds to her standing in one place, in the house, in chapter 5. And we are longing for Him, but it is Him who will come to us in yielded prayer in coming over the mountains. Only He knows the timing in prayer. Therefore it is depicted as we are standing at home in one place. On the inner, we are standing in one place. We are hungry; we are yielded into the deeper presence of Him where only His food can fill us. Only His love can fill us so that we are full so that the spiritual starvation is over. Here we see the growth in no longer waiting for Him to come over the mountain, but we want to go home with Him upon the mountains. Mountains are the spiritual high places in God, the heavenly sphere of the Lord, the merging in the intimate relationship. There is now a spiritual open door through which we know how to go. There is now growth for a deeper merging and not only waiting for Him; the waiting now becomes the merging because we now allow no personal agenda for His Spirit to move within. Standing in one place is also a direction of how we overcome the physical tribulation in prayer; the flesh is an influence that needs to be overcome. The yielding and waiting are the door for the Spirit to enter and overtake but now unable for the carnal to disturb; it is no longer in charge.

The waiting and yielding are pure worship; we turn to His face; we forget everything else; we love on Him, and He turns His cheek against ours. Then, the intimate inner love dance occurs, our eyes are closed, and we forget our problems or situations. In that, He takes care of them.

This absolute-impossible occurrence of dying in the flesh is one of the greatest mysteries because when we have once tried ourselves to calm down the flesh, we know what a miracle this is. This is by far one of the greatest gifts of Christ for us; dying to self, striving in the flesh in all matters and all areas of life. Then, finally, He kills us with His love; we die into His arms and are now a new living creation; living to live for Him; living for this Holy Communion in Christ Jesus.

*Elena Radef*

# Appendix

**Darkness and in the secret place**

In the secret place, it seems like darkness for the carnal man because he does not understand and perceive the ways of the Lord. Therefore, it brings fear to man, especially in the deeper ways of the Lord. When Jesus was walking on water, the disciples got scared. However, the Lord will always comfort us because He never leaves us abandoned not to understand. He wants us to understand. Otherwise, it would serve no purpose. But at first, it scares the carnal man because of the unfamiliarity. Then, however, the Lord will confirm His presence. Unfortunately, many people don't know of this matter with the Lord because the carnal man's approach is to take that which is familiar to be good and right, and that which it is unfamiliar, the secret place, to be wrong and disregard it. Especially in this matter way too soon, one misses the mark and depth of Jesus' heart.

Spiritually, the secret place is depicted as a small dark place as we read in: (Sg. 2:14) small, dark, unfamiliar, and uncomfortable for the flesh. In a small place, we cannot lie down but only stand up; in a ready spiritual position. We cannot see with the natural eyes; it is dark in a cleft; we must use the spiritual eyes; faith. There is not much we can do in a cleft; we must wait upon the Lord, pray, and yield. A cleft is also a place of protection that we first don't understand by heart, which is why it is depicted as a cleft and not a nice and beautiful place that we seemingly understand. The analogy here is that we don't understand the Lord's ways but must trust Him. The Bible describes this on different occasions: Moses (Exo. 33:22, 1 Kgs.19:13, Jer.13:4).

**Figs**

It means prosperity; He teaches us how to handle the blessings He proves over our lives; among others, the revelation of the fact that we are only stewards. He is the captain leading us where, when, and how to distribute the means regarding the outpouring of the blessing that He provides in our lives. It takes strength, endurance, and patience to handle a blessing from the Lord. The carnal is weak, and if not awake, it can easily fall into a trap by merely coming only to look upon the blessings and forgetting Him. By all means, we must remember that the carnal is weak.

## Garden

Resembles the church; the church is not a building filled with many people, it could be, but it also means the people we surround ourselves with. The church is where the Lord is positioning us to be. First, we must take into consideration that we are a church. Our life is a church; our body is the temple for God. First, He takes us through the purgation of cleaning us, transforming and teaching us to steer our own life through Christ. Then He can use us to lead, but first then. Only He knows when we are ready. He teaches us how to be led through the Holy Spirit and scripture. We see how Jesus led the disciples, how He talked, and why He said what He did in certain moments in time and places. How did He move through life, what did He do, and why? We must ask ourselves these questions, meditate and contemplate them. When we have received answers through revelation, we must ask again and go deeper because there is always more depth to be dug into because we constantly need to grow in Christ. All in order so that we can be of service to the people, and that implies church.

All the gifts in the church must be revealed individually and publicly because we each contribute with gifts from God. If one gift is not awakened through the purgation, then that one gift is missing in the church. A whole piece of bread is only whole when none of it is missing. Suppose each missing gift resembles a piece of that bread. In that case, one can see what happens if too many are not being instructed into becoming the body of Christ through the purgation into an awakened condition wherein the gifting can be of service for Christ in all.

## Milk and honey

They are often linked together when spoken of in the Bible. It is referred to as abundance, the sweetness of life, pure, wholesome, and true in relation to being referred to as a loved one's charms; one seeing and comprehending the love sprung out and forth from the other person. In that, we see the sweetness and love from the other person toward us; we recognize this pattern from the Lord toward us. He teaches us the love language, what we need to look out for, and what we need to tend to grow deeper constantly. Taken into the physical circumstances, He will show and lead us regarding the favor and blessings He is pouring upon our lives; we are merely stewards of everything that He provides. Milk symbolizes spiritually the rudiments of doctrine and the unadulterated Word of God, which fits very well regarding how the Lord is teaching us to grow to become more mature in Christ Jesus.

## Mountains

Overcoming our mountains, we all have big mountains that we cannot seem to turn around no matter how hard we try. From this, He teaches us how to turn the hindering mountains in us into becoming mountains ourselves. That means the mountains that used to suppress us, we now overcome by becoming mountains of Christ. The mountains are not to be taken lightly; it literally means illnesses, family problems, could be drugs, or other seemingly difficult problems, the conviction of crimes we never committed, life situations that are killing us, making us almost unable to live. Death is constantly lurking around the corner; financial problems we landed up in that seem to get worse and worse. He will guide us through all these mountains, walking in His footsteps in becoming His mountain.

## Pomegranates

The word pomegranate is derived from the Hebrew word *ramam*, which means to be exalted and rise up. Jewish traditions teach that the pomegranates symbolize righteousness because it is said to have 613 seeds, which correspond to the 613 commandments. The righteousness of Jesus was provided for us on the Cross. Yet we have to, in our purgation and the transformation into His image, receive the righteousness in every part of our soul; that comes within the understanding of what He did for us on the Cross. By this, we come to life, a renewed life in His image. Therefore, everything changes in our lives. We receive new desires; we receive His desires; by this, the old desires die. This is brought forth into every part of our being and soul: thinking, emotions, fantasies, imaginations, in speaking, our will, in our senses. Our life is turned around; we turn away from the old; it dies in the carnal man because of the purgation.

**Vine**

Jesus is the true vine from which the wine of life proceeds. It is the true vine because He gave Himself to us as the atoning sacrifice to redeem us once and for all. Thereby the blood became the most precious occurrence that has ever taken place. In Sacramenta, we are constantly being reminded of this occurrence. It is important that when we take Sacramenta, there is a certain and distinct spiritual change that takes place when we, in all humbleness and spiritual comprehension, take Sacramenta. It changes something within us, and it seems to be of a certain preciousness to the Father, and by this, certain attention is drawn to His holy act in remembrance of Christ when He gave Himself up. From this most precious act of Christ, wine becomes the metaphor for God's blessing because God was so well-pleased. The vine produces many grapes that will turn into much wine if we remain in Him and allow Him to prune us. A vine can only produce much and good wine when being pruned. We are the ones that the Lord chooses to let His wine flow through, bearing much abundant fruit. In pruning, there is blood that will be spilled. Jesus spilled His blood to produce much fruit, seemingly turning blood into the blessing of the wine.

He teaches us how to tend the vineyard and how to tend the relationship with Him. Each of us has a different calling, and we live in different times regarding countries and the timeline of the Bible. For each timeline we're in, certain actions need to be addressed to grow in that period of time. For

*Appendix*

example, Jesus was radical in His timeline and still is. This means the Lord will ask us to do things to display Himself in this time.

For example, a hundred years ago, a certain minister was asked not to wear a hat, which all men did at that certain period of time, but for us today, that would seem as if nothing. The Lord will ask us to do things that always lead to more freedom in Him, and the declaration of the chains of the world over our lives are broken, which Jesus provided on the Cross. However, He is making that display through us, which is why we must go through things and events in life. Our life is a constant declaration of the chains Jesus broke on the Cross and at the resurrection. In our relationship with Him, He teaches us how to nurture the relationship, the vine, in our walk with Him throughout every area of our life. John 15 depicts how to remain in Him. He constantly tells us. Only in Him do we know where, when, and how.

*Elena Radef*

For more information or requests email the publisher at:
info@advbooks.com

To purchase additional copies of this book, visit our bookstore website at:
www.advbookstore.com

"we bring dreams to life"™
www.advbookstore.com

www.ingramcontent.com/pod-product-compliance
Lightning Source LLC
Chambersburg PA
CBHW070702100426
42735CB00039B/2429